THE GOSPEL OF THE HOLY SPIRIT

The Gospel of the Holy Spirit

A Commentary on the Acts of the Apostles

ALFRED McBRIDE

Hawthorn Books, Inc.
W. Clement Stone, Publisher
New York

THE GOSPEL OF THE HOLY SPIRIT

Library of Congress Catalog Card Number: 75-217
ISBN: 0-8015-3098-9

1 2 3 4 5 6 7 8 9 10

Published by arrangement with Arena Lettres.

FOREWORD

"The Spirit is a movin' all over, all over this
land." . . . words of a familiar hymn that is rather
popular today and reflects a contemporary interest
and a new awareness of the presence of the Spirit in
the lives of Christians today.

In a sense it is a shame that we are in a period
of rediscovering the activity of the Spirit in the
Church. For this seems to imply that somewhere
along the line of maturation we have lost the awareness of his presence. There once was a time when
the activity of the Spirit among the Church was
considered to be "ordinary." Now we speak of the
gifts of the Holy Spirit as "extraordinary!" Why?
That question is a cause for great joy!

For it is with great joy that we acknowledge
that more and more books, articles, and talks have
as their theme the presence of the Spirit in modern
man's life. Even in conversation, one hears the
Spirit mentioned so much more today than in years
past.

The Gospel of the Holy Spirit, a commentary on
the Acts of the Apostles, is timely as well as helpful
for all Christians concerned with the development
of Christ's Church. The author, an articulate and
well-known religious educator, not only provides us
with a concise and helpful analysis on the workings
of the Spirit in the early Church, but makes the

Church of today "an offer that it cannot afford to refuse."

As one reflects on the Acts of the Apostles it seems clear that we see history repeating itself in many ways. The Church in the days of Peter and Paul felt the need to respond to the people of its time—there was need for change, which, like today, led to disagreements, contentions, and even apostasy.

It is quite clear in the Acts that there was need for healing, discernment, and reconciliation in the primitive Church, and we have a similar need today and will always have such a need as long as man has to struggle in this world with the force of evil.

McBride's book, written in contemporary style and language, can be read and pondered by all who desire to become more involved in the growth and development of the Christian Church. According to the author, "If no other lesson is learned from pondering the Bible's description of the growth of the Church, this one of the overriding presence of the Spirit must be assimilated."

Yes, the Spirit is a movin' all over, all over this land. May all of us be open and attentive to his inspirations.

Ronald A. Amandolare

CONTENTS

THE GOSPEL OF THE HOLY SPIRIT

INTRODUCTION

Religion works best when it recovers its contact with the Holy Spirit. Then believers understand really how to be doers of the word because they truly are hearers. They act from enthusiasm, a word that means "the God within."

Fortunately, a fresh experience of the Holy Spirit is widespread in the Church today. Were Ronald Knox alive, he would be adding another chapter to his book *Enthusiasm,* where he chronicles the many experiences of the Spirit throughout the history of the Church.

STRUCTURES

The gracious coming of the Spirit into our contemporary lives signals good news for many developments in the Church. As we work to design new structures to hold the new wine, we can take comfort that the organizational task of the Church will rest on the solid foundation of persons striving to be rich in spiritual experience. The organizational house can rise securely for the foundation is the rock of Christ.

COMMUNITY OF FAITH

Parishes and schools, engaged in building a "community of faith," are newly heartened to find they do not work alone. Humbly, we are gifted again with consciousness-raising from the Spirit as we come to see how we are able to rebuild communities of faith in our local parishes and schools. Jesus told the apostles at the Last Supper that he did not intend to leave us orphans. He would not consign us to the cold, for he promised to send the fire of the Spirit to quicken our imaginations, expand our narrow horizons and sweep away unnecessary chips from stubborn shoulders.

MISSIONARIES

Missionaries, too, are gaining their second wind from the mighty "breath of God" challenging them to renew the face of the earth. Far from being embarrassed by their new-found zeal, the Spirit-filled missionaries are caught up once again with St. Paul's graffito: "Woe to me if I preach not the Gospel of Christ." The obstacles are as great as any Paul ever faced. Paul faced the paganism of the Roman world. Today's missionaries face the grinding poverty and injustice of the Third World.

Paul struggled against the religious opposition of his former brethren. The modern missionary, similarly, often finds his former friends are sometimes the worst enemy to the people he tries to serve. Just as Paul fought to put each new local Church on its own feet, so his successors today aggressively struggle to help local Churches and cultures to find self-determination and independence. Prisons, beatings, hunger, shipwrecks and plane crashes face today's messenger of the Gospel. But the Spirit astonishingly fills these men and women with the ancient gift of "boldness" so they do not give up.

Thus the Spirit comes again to creators of Church organization, builders of community of faith and the mission worker to encourage, cajole, inspire, hearten, inflame and provoke. There is a future, a vision and a dream, woven in a jet-age style, but bearing the timeless message of Christ.

These are the kinds of themes that permeate the Acts of the Apostles, a biblical case study of our young Church in action. I call the story the "Gospel of the Holy Spirit" for Gospel is joyful news. And the best news here is that Christ's promise to give us his Spirit is fulfilled and here is the data to demonstrate it. In the Acts we find the first Christians building a Church from scratch. Every problem and every question is new. Yet, astoundingly, with almost every score against them, they succeed wildly. They do not take the credit. They confess plainly that the Spirit of Christ made it all possible.

They become a community of faith by the power of the Spirit at Pentecost. They gradually build Church structures—deacons, elders (priests), overseers (Bishops), prophets, teachers, administrators, healers, exorcists, wise ones—and firmly state that each of these developments is a charism, a gift of the Spirit.

They build a missionary network that would—without sounding irreverent—be the envy of any Japanese trade mission. How did they do it? Just with Roman roads? They leave us the testimony. If you walk by the Spirit you will live by the Spirit. Does Paul think up going to Macedonia on his own? If he did then he failed to let Luke know that. He says the Lord came to him and urged him to bring Christianity to Europe. They don't take the credit. They give God the glory.

A VERY HUMAN GROUP

This is not a method of discrediting their initiative, enthusiasm, energy, imagination, creativity or honesty. Peter and Paul and the disciples had plenty of this. Yet even knowing their own potential, they thought little of it, for they saw what great goals could be achieved when they allowed all of these talents to be put in touch with the ultimate fire.

They both loved the human and acted with a humanity that could delight a modern humanist. No one in Acts is a plaster ideal. When Paul flings a round curse at an establishment clergyman (Acts 23:3), and annoys the over-worked Alexandrian sailors with an I-told-you-so "You should have taken my advice" (Acts 27:21), and still sheds big tears at leaving his friends, saying "Why are you crying and breaking my heart in this way?" (Acts 21:13), he comes through as human as anyone could wish.

The people in Acts sing in jail, love a hearty meal, generously share their belongings, argue with lawyers and judges, tenderly care for (and heal) the sick, take up collections for the poor, debate religion with a passion, write numerous letters, devise cloak and dagger escapes, sail on perilous boat rides and pray with a simplicity and fervor that Christians ever since have envied. Yes, it's a very human community, and as they will tell you, it is because the Spirit fills their lives.

LUKE AS AUTHOR

We are more than blessed that it was Luke who came to write the Acts. He had already written a Gospel and so had sharpened his skill at telling a story. Actually Luke's Gospel and Acts are two parts of one book. When the books of the New Testament were being arranged in a sequence, it was decided to separate the Acts from the Gospel of Luke. The story of the Church should come after the four stories about Jesus.

A sense of unity is achieved by Luke's addressing both his Gospel and Acts to Theophilus. We don't know who this "god lover" is. But Luke, in doing this, adopts a Greek literary style and mannerism. Perhaps he did it so his work would have a special appeal to gentile readers. Luke was a doctor as well as a gifted writer. As a physician he would normally be more attentive to human detail than most people. This talent serves him well as he word-paints numerous vignettes to jog our imaginations and memories.

In the case of Acts, Luke is often an eyewitness of the events he describes. This becomes evident in the famed "we" passages that come up intermittently throughout the text. Perhaps his most vivid account, especially for a man who was not a sailor, occurs in his narrative of the shipwreck in chapter 27.

Luke names the book Acts of the Apostles. Acts obviously refers to actions, deeds, exploits, endeavors, enterprises, adventures and achievements of the persons talked about. It has an extra connotation in biblical and patristic (Church Fathers) literature, in that the supreme Act was martyrdom —dying for Christ.

Now while Acts at first appears to be about all the apostles, in fact most of it is written about Peter and Paul. The first 12 chapters concentrate mainly on Peter. This section could be called the book of Peter. The remaining 16 chapters might be termed the book of Paul. This is a convenient division, not a perfectly exact one. Paul appears in the first 12 chapters as a cooperator in the martyrdom of Stephen. Also the first story of his conversion appears in chapter nine. On the other hand, Peter makes an appearance in Paul's book, chapter 15, during the Apostolic Council in Jerusalem.

GRAND DESIGN

Luke writes Acts with a grand design in mind. He knows that at the Ascension Jesus wants the apostles to take the Gospel to the ends of the earth. Luke tells how this happened. He moves the story from the first flowering of the Gospel in Jerusalem, to its expansion in Antioch—from which missionary center it spreads to the gentiles first in Asia Minor, then over to Greece, and finally to Rome, "the end of the earth." The journey of the Gospel then, is from Jerusalem to Rome with many points in between.

Luke always keeps in mind the reason for this progress. Scarcely a paragraph or page goes by without a reference to the dynamic presence of the Spirit in the lives of the people who carry Jesus to the world. Every new development, every distinct growth is linked with its divine origin. Neither the scope of human nor divine power is ever cheated. Both are honored and integrated simply, directly and forcefully.

PREACHING

There is a great deal of preaching going on in Acts. Sermons, discourses, defenses, addresses and exhortations abound. Luke was not always present for all these talks. Hence he often had to rely on reports and summaries given to him. We must recall we are dealing with a largely oral-aural culture in which paper was not plentiful and the idea of instantly recording speeches was not the style.

The sameness of themes in many of the sermons, typical quotes from the Old Testament, applications to the work, passion and resurrection of Jesus, and the gift of the Spirit show that Luke is giving to us distilled memories of central addresses of the apostles. This may be why Paul's speeches in Acts do not sound as volcanic and bursting as his letters to the Churches. If Paul spoke as he wrote, then not even the most game reporter could move his stylus fast enough to get down the geysered cadences of the apostle. Hence, most commentators conclude that the sermons in Acts are reports of the substance of the preaching of the apostles, not necessarily blow-by-blow records.

In some instances this would be less true, as in the case of Peter's sermon at Pentecost, Stephen's martyrdom address and Paul's "Unknown God" talk at Athens. The special importance of these events probably caused a surer recall of the words than they would in other cases. This observation about the composition of the speeches in Acts will only be made here in the introduction and not referred to again in the commentary. It will be an assumption any time a sermon is reviewed.

The main thing to be remembered about the sermons is their evangelical character. This means they are talks that are aimed at changing both the mind and the heart of the listener. They are not neutral addresses. They present Jesus as necessary for the lives of people. The preachers offer information about Christ. For their Jewish listeners they build upon Old Testament references to help the audience see how Christ is a fulfiller of the Torah (Law of Moses).

But they always move beyond information. These speakers want to convert the listener. While the talks may sound argumentative in the sense that they seem to persuade by logic and good sense, the evangelists are quick to affirm that only the power of God can finally touch the hearts of the audience. Conversion is always a miracle of grace. This is self-evident to them from the moment they open their mouths, for they feel in their hearts the power of God's Spirit, and they know the Jesus they proclaim works to open the souls of the hearers.

The apostolic preachers realize that words do not just reflect reality, they also create it. This is what Isaiah meant when he wrote:

> "For just as from the heavens
>   the rain and snow come down
> And do not return there

till they have watered the earth,
  making it fertile and fruitful
Giving seed to him who sows
  and bread to him who eats,
So shall my word be
  that goes forth from my mouth;
It shall not return to me void
  but shall do my will,
  achieving the end for which I sent it

The proof of the pudding is certainly in the eating, for by all standards the apostolic sermons were enormously successful. They did convert people by the thousands, and in a comparatively short time spread Christianity to every major corner of the Roman Empire. Their example endures for the contemporary preacher who might have many different purposes in what he would like to accomplish. One thing is certain, conversion of heart to Christ remains one of them. He can take confidence from the Acts that such is possible so long as the discourse is within the horizon and power of the Spirit.

TONGUES

The gift of tongues appears so often in the first years of the Church that it is alluded to as practically an everyday event. The impression then is that it is a spiritual event taken for granted by the early believers. In Acts there is no thought that it might have any controversial or disturbing quality to it.

However, St. Paul does encounter questions about it from his Corinthian parishioners. He devotes chapters 12-14 to a discussion of the gifts (charisms) of the Holy Spirit. In chapter 12 he lists wisdom, knowledge, faith, healing, miracle working, prophecy and discernment. He spends all of chapter 13 on the gift of love which he names the greatest of all the gifts.

In chapter 14 he dwells on the gift of tongues. He speaks clearly in its favor. "Now I want you all to speak in tongues." (v.5) Apparently what has happened is that a good thing has been overdone. Fascination with the gift of tongues has evidently so captivated some of the groups that it is being used like a toy for self-gratification.

Paul then spends a good deal of time situating the gift in a larger context. The purpose of tongues is to lead toward a building up of the Church. Paul sets guidelines for the community that is having the difficulty. "If any are going to talk in tongues let it be at most two or three, each in turn, with another to interpret what they are saying. Let no more than two or three prophets speak, and let the rest judge the worth of what they say." (I Cor. 14:27-28)

This chapter must be read in the sense in which Paul means it. He is reacting to a topical problem, a local quarrel in the Corinthian Church. He sees tongues as a gift of the Spirit, but also sees the need for restrictions when it may be misused. His solution to the problem is not a law for all time, but an example of one way to approach a similar difficulty.

In our times psychologists have become interested in the phenomenon of tongues. They find it appears in many ecstatic situations. Usually it is discussed under its technical name *glossalalia*. From their perspective it is a symptom that often emerges in spiritualist groups whether Christian or otherwise. They tend to reduce the experience to a lesser form of subconscious eruption. Probably a psychic symptom and nothing more.

This is another example of the reductionist mind at work. Everything can be reduced to an explanation that will exclude the possibility of divine and spiritual influence. Doubtless there are times that tongues are of a purely psychic origin. Why should this exclude the possibility that there are also times that tongues are of divine and religious origin? In fact, why not? I have already alluded to the exuberant humanity of the people of Acts. Their universal testimony to tongues as a gift of the Spirit is quite persuasive, as is Paul's who is also objective enough to do his own critique of the "phenomenon."

HEALING

Another matter-of-fact event tirelessly reported in Acts is the gift of healing. This is truly "good-news Gospel" as much as is the preaching. Isaiah 35:5-6 foretold healing in the messianic age. From the very beginning of Acts to the end, healings are commonplace. In the last chapter, while Paul is resting at Malta before finally getting to Rome, he cures the father of the local island chief and then heals many others who come to him. Healing is seen as normal.

But the impulse of the reductionist, scientific mind is to reject this. People should go to doctors and psychiatrists and psychologists for their healing. Who is saying they shouldn't? The real question is, why should we forbid them to go to a believing healer? Maybe we could help lighten the case load of doctors and psychiatrists.

What Acts reminds us of is that healing is a gift of the Spirit. This means that the Christian believer who has the gift of healing is part of the "healing community." It is silly to reduce the question to a reductionist fantasy. "Well, maybe they do heal. But it's just psychosomatic illnesses. They would be far better off in the hands of certified doctors." Would they? Sometimes yes and sometimes, no.

I believe that the Christian with the gift of healing should work in communion with the medical and psychiatric community. This is becoming clearer in clinical pastoral ministry where the *mind* and *body* doctors are more ready now to welcome the *soul* doctors. Our goal is the full health of the patient—bodily, psychic and spiritual. Let's be friends, not absurdly suspicious enemies.

Obviously, I am not advocating fundamentalist behavior that leads to horror stories where the boy with the burst appendix dies because the doctor was not allowed to operate. What I am saying is that the teaching of Acts is clear, as is the teaching of the Church testified to in countless lives of saints in our own day, that healing is a gift of the Spirit, does occur in every age of the Church in greater or lesser extent, and should not be denied today because of some presumed enlightenment that makes it impossible. The world is sometimes too much with us. As Inge says, "He who marries the spirit of the age will soon be widowed." We need the bracing enlightenment of Acts to recall to our hearts some good news we may have forgotten.

EXORCISM

As in the Gospels, so in the Acts, the theme of exorcism occurs fairly often in the text. Sometimes it is associated with stories of apostolic encounters with magicians. The frequency of the magician tales should remind us that we are not the only age that has needed to cope with the occult. The Acts response to the occult is that it is a false reply to a genuine spiritual need. Our own response should be similar. The rise of the occult today reminds us that we are giving our young humanistics (in the bad sense) stones, instead of the bread of spiritual life.

Radical denial has a way of getting a vulgar come-uppance. Let us raise our children to deny the existence of evil spirits, or the so-called urbane variation: "They exist, but they cannot affect us either through temptation or possession." Well, we do this and then find ourselves facing a cinematic blockbuster, "The Exorcist," and are titillated and alternately ashamed that a monster film pushes demonic possession right back into the center of our urbanity.

I am frankly sorry that this happened. I do not believe that violent and sensational films should assault our sensitivities. But I can see how it happens. Massive denial gets massive response. We say it can't happen and then get nightmares about it due to a fictional account.

Here again the sobriety of the Acts is useful. Plainly the believers of the Acts thought possession could happen. They may not have been skilled to tell the difference between a psychosomatic state and true demonic possession. We think we can. The reason we are so smug is that so many of us say it's all psychosomatic, so of course we are good at judging. We haven't judged. We've simply pre-judged.

I am delighted that we have been able to share the burden of troubled psyches with mind-doctors. This is precisely the position of the Church. Happily we don't need instant exorcisms. We know now that many of the cases are due to epilepsy or a kind of hysteria or lesion of the temporal lobe. We just simply say there are times when this is not the case. Then bring in the exorcist. The lesson from Acts remains. There are evil spirits. They can influence us. Most of the time it is through temptation (Remember C. S. Lewis' "Screwtape Letters"?) and more rarely, through possession.

DISCERNMENT

This discussion leads us to another fine gift so prominent in Acts, namely, that of discernment. The real reason for reductionist thinking, whether of the religious fundamentalist or the collapsed humanist, is that both groups are too lazy to bother trying to discern, that is, to sort out the case. They suffer from the indolence of extremes. It is easy to decide ahead of time that certain things can't happen. Then, of course, they won't. Or so we imagine.

Naturally, we expect this of fundamentalists since social surveys tell us they are of a poorer, less educated (and presumably unintelligent) class of people. It's hard for us to see this is an elitist judgment, until we take a second look at the elite who seem quite capable of a hearty dose of close-mindedness themselves in some instances. The 18th century elite prided themselves on being an age of reasoners. But then it was very embarrassing for the English elite to stumble on Satan cults in their country estates and London townhouses. It was even more disconcerting for the French elite to find themselves attending a black mass right in the king's court.

Instead of a denial there should have been discernment. The human mind is perfectly capable of discernment, that is, making wise and perceptive

judgments about the events of life and the expres-
sions of people. The Acts candidly ascribe discernment to a gift of the Spirit. Nowhere was this more
dramatically evident than in the story of the Apostolic Council as described in chapter 15.

The issue of circumcision was tearing the Church
apart. The reductionist elite (some Jewish converts) were arguing that gentiles must be circumcised before baptism and acceptance into the
Church. The debate raged on and on. Position
papers flew. Authorities were cited. Mighty men
spoke. But the Church realized there was more to
all this than the rhetorical flourishes of advocates.

"The whole assembly fell silent." (v.12)

There is a time for listening to more than oneself. There is a moment in which we must ask life
what it is not yet telling us. We must beg the Spirit
to reveal to us the "not yet." We should humbly
admit that we are experts at the half-vision and
need the light from the fountain of truth itself. Discernment is a gift to be prayed for. Acts makes it
clear they did pray for discernment, and what is
more, they received it. The decree of the Apostolic
Council led the way for the evangelization of the
gentiles and the gift of Jesus to all men.

Now this is not to say that the task of reasoning
is to be abandoned, that meditative prayer will
solve everything. Not at all. Thinking is also a gift
of God and ought to be used. I am speaking against
its misuse, that is when reason becomes so sure of
itself that it begins to create a smaller universe that
forbids entry to healing and exorcism because it is
so afraid of lapses into superstition and barbarism.
There is no need for this fear when the fuller picture is seen. The advocates at Jerusalem knew how

to reason and argue. Mercifully, they also knew how to pray.

Let us not only listen to ourselves, but also to being, to the Spirit trying to get through to us.

BOLDNESS

There are those who have said that courage is one of the best proofs for the existence of God. If that be so, then it is no small wonder that Acts is a story that reminds one of God's presence. Over and over again the main characters in Acts display boldness and courage. Luke says this is also a gift of the Spirit. It signifies both a resounding conviction in their preaching and a stirring bravery in the face of dangers and death.

I will expand on this in the commentary since it occurs so frequently. Let it suffice to say here that today we are no less in need of courage and boldness to put soul in our faith, convictions and moral fiber in our ethical lives. We should turn to the Holy Spirit for this gift as did our first brothers and sisters in the faith.

FROM KINGDOM TO CHURCH

Acts will be better understood if we realize that all the first Christians were Jewish converts. They were people steeped in the love of the Torah, fond of the great feasts which they had known since childhood, and totally of the cultural mind set of a devout Jew—and one who lived in Palestine at that. The movement from Judaism to a distinctly separate and new Church took some time. Jesuit commentator, David Stanley, uses the expression "from kingdom to Church."

In the beginning they are the free spirited kingdom of God come true. They are born in the shadow of the Temple, still pray in it even as they celebrate the joyous meal of the Eucharist in their homes and shout from their worship table, "Maranatha!", come Lord Jesus. They will become a distinct Church in due time. If you want to label a time period for the "weaning," it would be from Pentecost in A.D. 33 to the destruction of the Temple in A.D. 70.

During their kingdom period they think of themselves as the perfectly fulfilled Judaism—but still Judaism. The Torah has found realization in the life of Jesus, the sacraments of Baptism and Eucharist and in the community of believers. At first even the Jewish leaders concur. They think the Nazarenes are troublesome but still brothers. Soon they stretch the troublesomeness to accusations of heresy. No longer mainstream Judaism, but now a sect.

You will find Paul in the latter part of Acts stressing the continuity side of Christianity with Judaism. He does this as a strategy both to urge the Jewish community to accept Christ by seeing that their own beliefs should lead to Jesus, and he also wishes to throw the cloak of Roman imperial protection, which already guards the rights of Judaism, over the Christian group.

Luke carefully outlines the successive shocks which disengage the Christians from their Jewish matrix. The conversion of the gentile Cornelius, Phillip's conversion of the Ethiopian, Paul's own conversion and mission to the gentiles, the opening of a central mission station for the gentiles at Antioch, the missionary journeys of Paul, the settling of the circumcision question at the Apostolic Council and the progressive and serious breaks with the synagogue communities in every corner of the empire all lead to the realization that Christianity must come to see itself as a radically new religion, a Church that is no longer in direct continuity with Judaism (or a fulfillment group within the Jewish fold).

Yet even with all this psychological and official disengagement, the immemorial ties with the ancient religion continue. Four years before he dies Paul makes one last pilgrimage to the Temple, spends seven days in retreat according to the rites of Nazarite purification and definitely wishes to avoid alienating his one-time co-religionists. Deep differences have arisen, but his love and reverence for the religion of the patriarchs abides. This is the kind of attitude echoed today when Pope John met with Jewish leaders and welcomed them with the words, "I am Joseph, your brother."

RELIGIOUS EXPERIENCE

One of the striking teachings of Acts is that being flooded with the Spirit of God is central to whatever else happens, be it organizing the Church, knowing what community means or sending forth the missionaries. In modern terms this is also called religious experience. There is a tendency to look at religious experience at the phenomenal level. This means it is interpreted only in terms of how people feel when they have one.

Again this is too limited a view. Oceanic dizziness, ecstatic wonder and interior exaltation is not the whole point at all. It's not so much how one feels, but what it means for one's life and for the Church and the world. The Acts never comment on the feeling at all. The text notes that the Spirit manifests himself in wind and fire. The people begin to speak in tongues, preach, heal, exorcise, build community, discern, love, teach, prophesy and die for their belief. Their religious experience moves quickly from the event of Spirit shock to the types of behavior just mentioned.

Furthermore, all of this is not seen as unusual, but quite normal. They don't seem to think of themselves as odd mystics so much as proper and sensible heirs of what Jesus was all about. What's abnormal is not sharing in and enjoying the event of the Spirit and the consequences. Those people knew instinctively what we may have to learn consciously, namely, that God made our hearts to stretch out to nothing less than the infinite and that he is graciously waiting for us to look and listen so he can answer and come.

They touched the Lord at the point of his love. That's what gave them the daring to speak up before princes and kings, to charm an empire into the kingdom of Christ, to die courageously for one they loved and knew they were loved by in turn. Do you remember how Romeo tells Juliet he was so skillful in reaching her despite all obstacles? "With love's light wings, I did o'er perch these walls. For walls cannot keep love out. And that which love dare do, that will love attempt."

The early Christians had the good grace to let down their guard, their walls, so the flight of the Spirit into their marrow and bones was totally successful. In turn they turned the fire of that love on an alienated world which was only too ready to open its arms in welcome. When Jesus met the Samaritan woman at the well of Jacob, he was meeting a lonely and suspicious woman. She had been hurt too much. Five lovers had disappointed her and left her life in ruins. Jesus brought her then what she thought was no longer possible. She ached for salvation. Jesus said, "Woman, I who speak

with thee am the one." And then she knew. Her
dream of becoming whom she was meant to be, a
person generously and infinitely loved, came true.
Only God could make it happen. And he did. That
was the incredible religious experience of the
Church of Acts. That is the astonishing grace available yet to us today.

That Church touched God at the point of his
wisdom. Where did the eloquence come from that
evoked a river of words recorded in the speeches of
Acts? The book of Genesis says that when God
spoke, man was able to talk. "Let man be!" Then
man was and spoke and acted. It is the same with
mothers and babies. Mothers speak. Babies listen
and learn how to talk and act. In Acts the Spirit
speaks and fires the Church to speak with boldness
the Word of God. Religious experience touches the
fountains of language and creates the poetry and
message that is destined to sway the human heart
and call men to know their profound vocation.

One of the first results of religious experience in
Acts is the creation of community. Today we speak
of the need for community. We fail to make a central distinction. We need to differentiate organization from community. Normally man makes organi-
zations. That is God's gift to us, to give our minds
the wisdom to figure out how to govern ourselves.
But God makes community. Community is always a
gift, a grace and a miracle.

We will read those beautiful passages in Acts
that describe the ideal community. Regrettably—
but how realistically—we shall also read about de-
fections in community as in the case of Ananias and
Sapphira. If we find our own groups full of divisions then we know we have modern versions of the
Tower of Babel. We must, in such cases, search for

and beg forth from the Spirit the gift of community.

A second result of religious experience is words, both revelational and humanistic. Glorious experiences in our hearts will always mean prophetic words on our lips. When the Blessed Virgin was full of her religious experience, namely Jesus, she went to visit her cousin Elizabeth. Thomas Merton writes of this in his poem, "The Quickening of John the Baptist." He sees her going off to Ain Karim to visit her cousin. "Woman, why are your clothes like sails?" But she rushes onwards to help her cousin.

When she meets Elizabeth, the presence of Jesus within her prompts John, present in Elizabeth, to kick in ecstasy, to have a religious experience. Merton writes, "O John (and therefore all who know God) your ecstasy is your apostolate, for whom to kick is contemplata tradere." This Latin expression means that the impact of God in prayer and religious experience should result in passing the fruits and effects onto the Church and the world.

It is then that Mary sends those unforgettable words out to the mountains in her magnificat. "My soul thrills with the Lord . . ." Her words are revelational as are all the words of Scripture, the Creeds of the Church, the dogmas, and the basic teachings. If we meet the Lord why shouldn't we tell about it. The speeches in Acts are just such an expression.

I mention that humanistic words are as well a result of religious experience. This means that all human learning ultimately is attributable to God in the sense that he gave us an intelligence to use and the potential to reach the discoveries that are so good for human development today.

A final result of religious experience is structure. The prophet Amos says that in the final days of the world the mountains will flow with wine. "Behold the days are coming, says the Lord . . . The mountains shall drip sweet wine and all the hills shall flow with it." (Amos 9:13). Jesus gave that prophecy special fulfillment at the miracle of wine at Cana. The Spirit made it a special possibility in the Pentecost event.

The problem for us is to find new wineskins, new structures to make sure that the wine of the Spirit is not lost, but saved and conserved for our time. There seems to be no question that we are reliving once again the Acts of the Apostles. A new Pentecost is upon us. The Vatican Council signaled a fresh outpouring of the Spirit in our midst. The grace of universal religious experience in the Church has come. We have known the joy, now we must know the discipline and the effort needed to make the appearance of the Spirit take a solid and permanent shape in our institutions and structures. We certainly are capable of creating the new wineskins which shall enable future generations to know and experience our glorious union with God even as we look back in history to the Exodus and to the passion and resurrection of Christ and share in the exaltation of those events of long ago.

A COMMENTARY

The following material is a commentary on the Acts. I have decided to keep it from being very technical. I have made no references to foreign languages, though some of my conclusions are the results of such references. Every attempt has been made to present the material as a flowing story and continuous narrative. Acts happens to be one of the most exciting stories in the Bible, so my task is made much easier by an inherently interesting tale.

As I mentioned earlier, I am assuming that the speeches in Acts are to some extent summaries and reports rather than word by word accounts. I believe that my position on tongues, healings, exorcisms should be sufficiently clear by now. I do not follow a reductionist theory of these events, nor do I consider myself a fundamentalist in these matters.

I truly feel that a serious and prayerful meditation on the Acts would be beneficial for the Church today. The young Church in action is a marvelous stimulant for the historic Church that wants to get into action in the late 20th century. Given the fact that relevancy is so popular a mood today (even with nostalgia) it is astonishing how "relevant" Acts is for our current self understanding.

I know that in working on this material, my own faith was touched, my own hopes were deepened, and my sense of a positive future was awakened in a way that can only be spoken of as gift. I offer you this experience of the Spirit who has been so generous to me.

1 COME HOLY SPIRIT

PREFACE 1:1—5

Luke addresses his work to Theophilus whose name means "lover of God." Previously, Luke also had addressed his Gospel to Theophilus. This literary device, popular among cultured Greeks, indicates the unity of Luke-Acts and is meant to appeal to the educated of the day. The risen Jesus spends forty days with his apostles, dwelling on the meaning and reality of the Kingdom of God. The subject of the kingdom is the original message of both John the Baptist and Jesus at the Jordan river.

The point here is that the message of the earthly Jesus and that of the Risen Lord is precisely the same. The life and power of God is available through faith, conversion and a baptism that startles the consciousness to the reality of the Spirit's indwelling.

ASCENSION 1:6—11

The apostles' question about the Kingdom of God shows they still think of it in terms of politics. It is also reminiscent of their earlier queries about the destruction of the Temple and the end of the world. As he did before, Jesus again leaves the time of disclosure wrapped in mystery.

The important thing is that they possess a radical openness to the coming of the Spirit who will flood them with power and courage to be his witnesses to all the world. The mentioning of the sequence Jerusalem, Judea, Samaria and the end of the earth, which will mean Rome, is a forecast of the actual way the Church expanded. The apostles must assimilate the "great expectation of the Spirit." In so doing they will loosen their resistance to the real kingdom of God, namely, the dynamic power of the Spirit.

The account of the Ascension echoes Easter. While clouds of glory image the exaltation of Jesus, two angels, as they had done at the tomb, advise the apostles to quit staring into emptiness. Jesus is no longer behind them, but ahead of them, awakening their hopes and expectations and urging them to rediscover him in the gift of the Spirit.

So they make their Sabbath's day journey (one half mile) back to the Upper Room in Jerusalem. In that Eucharistic chamber, along with Mary, the mother of Jesus, and with other brethren—120 in all—they enter into prayer and retreat, gradually opening their hearts to the power of the Spirit.

ELECTION OF MATTHIAS 1:15–26

The tragic history of Judas is reviewed. The 30 pieces of silver are used to buy a burial ground for strangers. They name the place "the field of blood." Matthew (27:3-10) has the priests buying it, while Luke asserts Judas had purchased it. In any event, Judas commits suicide and his money cloaks the purchased field with the blood memory.

The election of Matthias offers Peter an opportunity to define an apostle as one who had been an eyewitness of the historical and risen Jesus and had participated with him in the ministry of the Word. Paul modifies that definition, declaring that he is a real apostle so long as he, too, is a witness of the risen Christ, even though not of the historical Jesus. In passing we should note that the ministry of the original 11 apostles plus Matthias had been confined to the Jewish community, while Paul had carried the Word to the gentiles. The word apostle is from the Greek *angellos* meaning messenger.

2 A MIGHTY WIND AND FIRE

PENTECOST 2:1—13

In Jewish liturgy Pentecost was the feast of Mount Sinai. It celebrated the giving of the ten commandments to Moses and the sealing of the covenant of God with his people. A mighty wind and fire swept the slopes of Sinai evoking the awesomeness of the moment. The wind was the breath of God and the source of all life. The fire was his glory manifesting his presence to people.

The Exodus was the first decisive act of love of God for Israel. A testing period of forty years, during which the people made a pilgrimage from the waters of the Red Sea to the foot of Sinai, preceded this second critical deed of love. Now in the transcendent ceremony of Sinai, God finalized the pledge of his love for Israel.

The Upper Room of the Christian Pentecost is a new Sinai. Once again the mighty breath of God and the fire of his presence sweeps through the human community. Just as Easter had been a new Exodus illustrating a decisive act of love, not just for one people, but for all mankind, so now Pentecost is a new Sinai in which the Spirit of God is set as a seal on the whole universe—a declaration of irrevocable love for all people.

They were filled with enthusiasm (a word which means the God within) and experienced ecstasy (a word which means standing outside oneself). They knew the seizure of the Spirit. The Bible has many accounts of God seizure. Note the story of Samson. His friends bind him with ropes and betray him to his enemies, the Philistines, as a hostage to stop war. His captors torment and taunt him beyond reason. Hence "the Spirit of the Lord came upon him: the ropes around his arms became as flax that is consumed by fire." (Judges 15:14)

With such Spirit power, Samson seizes the jawbone of an ass and slays a thousand Philistines of this world. "With the jawbone of an ass, I have piled them in a heap, With the jawbone of an ass I have slain a thousand men." (Judges 15:16)

A further account of Spirit seizure occurs in the story of Daniel imprisoned in the lion's den. The prophet languished there six days without food. God noted the hunger of Daniel and relieved him through the services of the prophet Habakkuk.

"In Judea there was a prophet, Habakkuk; he mixed some bread in a bowl with the stew he had boiled, and was going to bring it to the reapers in the field, when an angel of the Lord told him, 'Take the lunch you have to Daniel in the Lions' den at Babylon.' But Habakkuk answered, 'Babylon, sir, I have never seen, and I do not know the den!' The angel of the Lord seized him by the crown of his head and carried him by the crown of his hairs, with the speed of the wind, he set him down in Babylon above the den." (Daniel 14:33-36)

These Old Testament stories of the seizure of the Spirit argue that such events were intermittent, rare and happened only to special people. The story of Pentecost and the remainder of New Testament teaching maintain that the seizure of the Spirit is a normal experience of the members of the Church. Such occasions are not meant to be rare, but rather the daily bread of Christians.

One hundred and twenty people were gathered in that Upper Room at Pentecost. According to the law of Israel, this was the number needed for an official liturgical gathering. It was a classical number for the ideal worshipping community. It was in the midst of their prayer and worship that they knew decisively the power of God's Spirit.

They began speaking in tongues (glossalalia) a language phenomenon that sometimes accompanies profound spiritual experience. Armed with the fire of the Spirit, and with ecstatic speech on their lips, they flowed out of the Upper Room into the square where pilgrims from over fifteen nations were gathered for religious observance. The crowd responded with positive astonishment, negative cynicism and finally honest truth searching.

In wonder, the crowd vibrated happily with the contagious enthusiasm and excitement of the Spirit-filled community and they identified with the linguistic miracle. There was a fleeting moment when the nations of the earth paused from their strife and profound community took place.

The artists of the Middle Ages loved to contrast the babbling and alienated mob of Babel's tower to the loving, linguistically united community by the tower of the Upper Room. Babel symbolized the fundamental divisions of people caused by selfishness and sin. Pentecost stood for the glorious assurance that such division was no longer a tragic necessity of mankind. The seizure of the Spirit was a guarantee that the horizons of human unity are not merely a dream, but an achievable reality.

But such unity was not easily won, and certainly not by human vision alone. After the first glow, some in the crowd began, defensively, to accuse the apostles of being drunkards. Still, that was an insufficient response. Taunting gave way to questioning. "What does this mean?" It was Peter who replied.

PETER'S DISCOURSE 2:14–41

This is the first missionary sermon. It is addressed only to Jews. Peter says that his people are not drunk because it is too early in the morning (third hour = 9 A.M.). Like any good rabbinical preacher, Peter fortifies his opening argument with an authoritative citation from the Scriptures, in this case, the prophet Joel.

Joel predicts that in the final age of mankind the Spirit will be available to everyone. The Spirit experience will be normative in our global village. The visions of the young and the dreams of the old mean the same thing, namely, a God-given insight into the real meaning of life. The imagery of Joel, with its blood soaked moons and blackened suns, is a poetic way of describing an age in crisis. Such a crisis should precipitate basic questions about ultimate meaning. The wonder of Pentecost is a crisis event calling people to abandon superficial reflection and come to probe the deep things of God.

Once Peter has established that Joel's prophecy is finding fulfillment today, he proceeds to show how that foresight takes shape in the person and ministry of Jesus. Every missionary from this moment on will follow Peter's example. The call to conversion can only be in terms of adherence to the person and work of Jesus. Cultural preliminaries may indeed be brought to bear, as Paul will show in his Athenian preaching, where he builds up to Jesus by first designating the implications of Greek poets, singers and philosophers and seeing them as the condition for the possibility of understanding the Lord.

Peter's talk on Jesus is the classical bare-bones of the Christian message. God does many mighty works and wonders through him during his ministry. An innocent lamb, he is delivered to death. But God shall not let him remain in the bonds of death. Then, with a touch of preacher's drama, Peter gestures toward the tomb of David and quotes from the 16th psalm, "You will not abandon my soul to the nether world, nor will you suffer your faithful one to undergo corruption." Obviously, David's body had seen corruption. Hence, it must be a text that applies to the expected Holy One, the Messiah, who is the Jesus that Peter preaches.

God has raised up his son Jesus and placed him at his right hand. David also speaks of Ascension in psalm 110, "The Lord said to my Lord, sit at my right hand." David did not ascend, but Christ did and has sent the Spirit who has caused the marvels which arouse such ardent inquiry on this day. Thus the substance of preaching Jesus includes the disclosure of God's prodigious actions in his son, the redeeming passion and death and the saving power of the resurrection and exaltation—all of which appears now in Christ's Spirit.

Jesus is thus Lord and Christ. The word *Lord*, normally meant to apply to political sovereigns, now testifies to Christ's reign over all the universe. The term *Christ* signifies Messiah.

Peter's sermon shakes his listeners. He is not preaching a detached recitation of dry facts, but rather a personal testimony designed to change the hearts of his listeners. Peter had much more at stake than presenting a neutral view of Christ. His own soul now knows the glory, and he is anxious that all the world should share his own vision and joy. Good news in the heart calls for a compelling message on the lips.

Small wonder then the listeners say they are pierced to the heart. Peter's talk had served as a supreme consciousness-raiser, driving to the surface the fundamental thirst that God plants in all human hearts. This is no whiling away the hour with curious discourse. People's lives are at stake and the course of future history is the gamble of this hour. Thus the central question takes shape, and the cry is heard on all sides, "What shall we do?"

Peter calls for repentance. This word basically means conversion. It is not as easy to appreciate in our day which favors the psychological view of gradual and developmental decision making. Striking decisions and radical conversions are somewhat out of fashion. One ought to resist any temptation to such breathtaking and daring commitments. Our prejudice is to pre-analyze away such possibilities.

The slogan is, "Leave your options open." This approach is not without its own wisdom. But when it is exaggerated to the point that decisive options are never taken, that every imaginable avoidance technique is used to defend against any crisis that would provoke such a decision, then Peter's call is not going to make much sense.

It is popular in some religious circles to speak of radical commitment. Yet an examination of those who propose this often uncovers the sad fact that fear and timidity, under the guise of psychologically prudent caution, has canceled the adventurous daring that commitment implies. But as Peter says, the gift of the Spirit stands before every human heart promising the greatest human fulfillment that any person can really know. Certainly the God who made the fiber of man, knows how to summon every nerve to its out-reaching hope.

Peter's admonition, "Save yourselves from this crooked generation," rings uncannily true in our time when values can find no honored place in the public order. The example of that first congregation should be an inspiration to the possible hearers of the Word today. On that first great day, three thousand opened their hearts to God's Spirit, and celebrated the event with Baptism.

THE GREAT COMMUNITY 2:42–47

The isolation, loneliness and alienation of modern people could find great hope in the communal effect of the Spirit upon the lives of the first converts. They touched the Spirit at the point of his love and found how sweet and good it was to reach out to others and know the marvelous joy of community. They touched the Spirit at the point of his wisdom and drank in the basis of all the religious teaching that poured out from the apostles. As love bound their hearts, wisdom united their minds so that as Augustine would say later to his community of priests at Hippo, "They were of one mind and heart in God."

They found in the "breaking of the bread," an expression for the Eucharist and in their prayers a divine celebration of their new-found lives and a further enrichment and strength for its future possibilities. God's boisterous love had prayed them from their dullness. Now their enthusiastic prayer prayed forth God's continuing gift of himself in the Spirit.

The text says that "fear" had come upon them. This must be understood in terms of awe and reverence. It is not a fright so much as a wonder that stirs them to hold their gift gingerly. Anyone who is "by love possessed" knows what fear really means in such a situation. No longer are they terrorized by an angry law-giver, for they are in contact with generous and unending love for the first time in their lives. In our own idiom we might be prompted to say, "What a way to wake up in the morning"!

It is clear that the Spirit prompted them to live the common life. They sell their possessions and share all things in common. Their prayer life alternates between the Temple and the home. It may seem odd at first to us that they continue to go to the Temple, but we must recall that no great opposition between the Temple and their new life had yet occurred, though, of course, it would happen soon enough. Still, even with that, they had had no reason to forsake the ancient hours of prayer which their ancestors from time immemorial had offered at the Temple, and which Jesus himself had been faithful to throughout his life.

In a sense, the Temple served as a kind of intermediate stage, a kind of cocoon, while the infant Church formed itself into an independent structure. Once the Temple was destroyed and its shadow, both comforting and possibly restricting, was removed, then the new people of God sensed quite clearly their identity. Of course, other elements facilitated this as well, especially the circumcision controversy as we shall see.

The natural locale for the Eucharist was the home and would remain so in all New Testament accounts, and indeed for some centuries until Constantine offered Christians basilicas for Eucharist. The setting of a home evoked a special style for liturgy. Of necessity it was more informal, though never irreverent—at least in the ideal. Paul would comment on unruly house liturgies in Corinth. (I Cor. 11:22)

The house liturgy urged the president of the Eucharist to be skilled in the art of hospitality, for of all tables, that of the Lord should evoke the warmest of welcomes. Obviously this kind of celebration testified to the closeness of God to the people. It spoke of his immanent presence to creation. Later on, the majestic Churches would witness to God's transcendence, his otherness from creation. Both witnesses are necessary for a real appreciation of God.

If there is only his closeness, then there is a familiarity that breeds banality. We reduce God to our size. If there is only his distance, then we find it too difficult to imagine he is real and interested in us, and so we reduce him to an unimportant something on the edge of the real world.

In the first flush of the ideal community, the breaking of the bread rode this tension well.

3 THE HEALING SERVANT

CURE OF THE LAME MAN 3:1–10

To this point we have seen that the impact of the Spirit resulted in strong, effective preaching, considerable conversions, the emergence of common life centered around the breaking of the bread. The next major result of the Spirit's influence was the power of healing. Jesus said that he came to bring good news (Gospel) and then went on to do a great many healings, which were certainly good news indeed to the happy recipients.

Now Peter and John, suffused with the Spirit of Jesus, realize their healing possibilities. They have gone up to the Temple for the 3 P.M. (ninth hour) prayer service. They come to the beautiful gate where a well-known cripple had kept his begging space. The lame man does not ask for a cure, not even realizing that he could. He simply makes his customary plea for alms.

The two apostles don't reach for their purses. Instead they give him a searching look and insist that he pause and take a good look at them. This is to be no ritual asking and giving of a donation. He hears Peter tell him that he has no money, but something far greater, the power to heal his lameness. Peter heals the man "in the name of Jesus." This will anger the local authorities and be the occasion of the first opposition to the new community.

The lame man at first doesn't quite realize what is happening. So Peter takes him by the hand and raises him to his feet. When he finds that he is able to walk, he literally jumps for joy. He accompanies the apostles into the Temple, "walking, jumping about and praising God."

The act of healing through the power of the Spirit was a very strong practice in the early ages of the Church. As the centuries wore on its scope narrowed to the lives of the saints and certain miracle centers like Lourdes. It took the form of "faith healing" in some of the Protestant sects.

Today there is a renewed interest in the power of healing as a more normal part of Church life—and not the exception which recent centuries have indicated. As this more sober, yet deeper, understanding of healing develops, the good news aspect of Gospel, which was so prevalent in the early

Church, will take on a remarkably positive realization for the community of believers in our own age.

PETER EXPLAINS THE MIRACLE 3:11–26

The excitement generated by the miracle forces Peter to stop by Solomon's Portico (the eastern side of the Temple) and tell the people of its meaning. Luke adds a visual note that the healed man clings to the arms of Peter and John as the sermon progresses.

The central point of Peter's message is that the theology of the cross was operating here. He compels their attention to the passion of Christ in order to gain access to the reason for the miracle. He knows they will understand this idea best by relating Christ's passion to that of the story of the suffering servant described in the poems of Isaiah.

That prophet had written four poems describing a man who would be simply designated as the "Servant of God." Three elements would mark his life. (1) He would be anointed by the Spirit of God. "Upon whom I have put my Spirit." (Is. 42:1) (2) He would fight for justice and bring healing. "Until he establishes justice on the earth . . . Upon him was the chastisement that makes us whole, by his stripes we were healed." (Is. 42:4; 53:5) (3) He will go so far as to die to bring this about. "Like a lamb led to slaughter, he was cut off from the land of the living and smitten for the sin of his people." (Is. 53:7,8,5)

Healing would be a principle act of the servant. He comes to "bring glad tidings to the lowly, to heal the brokenhearted, to proclaim liberty to the captives and release to the prisoners. To announce a year of favor from the Lord." (Is. 61:1-2) Jesus applies these thoughts to himself in the beatitudes.

Certainly he refers to himself when he speaks of the joy of the man who is persecuted and endures all manner of evil against him for the sake of the kingdom.

The self-disclosure of Jesus in the beatitudes identifies him as the one who comes to accomplish what Isaiah speaks to a community of hope. The passion narratives of the Gospel clearly show Jesus as the servant-lamb who by his free and willing acceptance of death made the possibility of justice ultimately come true.

Peter could count on his listeners knowing about the theme of the servant, the holy martyr who brings healing and justice. He also knew that they were aware of the recent history of the life and passion of Jesus. The suffering of Jesus and his consequent resurrection released the healing power of the Spirit so evident at that moment in the joyful face of the cured lame man.

To reinforce the whole argument, Peter cites Moses' prediction that there would come again a prophet like himself, namely, a savior figure who would proclaim and enact a theology of liberation far superior than even Moses would have imagined. Peter flatly states that Jesus is that prophet like Moses, only more so.

As in his first missionary sermon, Peter aims at conversion. Forcefully, he confronts them with the typical reaction of people to prophetic utterance. They don't listen. Yet Moses said, "You shall listen to him in everything he says to you." (Acts 3:22) Peter is anxious to shake up his hearers so they can truly be hearers of the Word.

4 THE BOLDNESS OF COMMON MEN

DEFENSE BEFORE THE SANHEDRIN 4:1—22

Peter gets no chance to finish the call to conversion because the captain of the Temple and the Sadducee delegation arrest him and John. The reasons for the arrest are that the two men are usurping the official teaching position of the religious professionals, and worse yet, they are proclaiming resurrection from the dead, a doctrine roundly denied by the Sadducees.

Still, though Peter was not able to complete his summons to conversion, he was later pleased to learn that 2,000 more converts were, in fact, made, bringing the total number of Christians to 5,000. Paul was later, gloomily, to say that the mission to the Jews utterly failed. This was not so, as the first 12 chapters of Acts was to testify; for the Church was well established in the Jewish communities in Jerusalem, Judea and Samaria. Paul was probably thinking more of his own lack of success with the diaspora Jewish communities in the gentile world.

The two apostles were brought before alumni of the office of high priest, among whom the senior member was Annas. He had been high priest from A.D. 6-15. Five of his sons were subsequently to hold that high office. Why the apostles were brought before this particular group is not clear, except they must have had in some way the legal power to prosecute.

Though the ostensible reason for the arrest is the question and content of their teaching, their interrogation is about the healing. Peter, as the national leader, makes the response. Luke notes that Peter speaks as an inspired man, "filled with the Holy Spirit." He repeats the substance of his sermon at Solomon's Portico, namely, that it had been in the name of Jesus, the holy Servant of God, that the healing had been possible.

He reminds them that they are the agents of Christ's crucifixion, but that they should know that just as this lame man, numbed in the death of paralysis, now joyfully is risen from his affliction, so is Jesus loosened from the bonds of death and raised into glory. Peter's use of the image of the cornerstone is a popular theme from the psalms and often used in religious exposition.

If you don't have a cornerstone, your building hasn't got much of a future. If you decide to reject Jesus as the cornerstone of God's relations with people, your religious hopes are futile. Standing so near the mighty stones of the Temple of Solomon, the image acquires a special rhetorical resonance. Peter drives home the message. There is no salvation in anyone else but Jesus.

Luke writes that they were overwhelmed by the "boldness" of these two men. How could uneducated, untrained and such "common" men be able to speak so eloquently and with such obvious force. They know that Peter and John had been companions of Jesus. Certainly Christ had performed a remarkable training job on these two men. They are unable to see what it means to have the Holy Spirit flooding one's consciousness and endowing the heart with transcendent courage and the mind with a clear eyed articulation of the basic message.

The priests confer together as to what to do with these men. Strangely, they do not call for an end to the work of healing. Rather they prohibit any further activities in the area of teaching. They put a ban on talking about Jesus. Peter and John, however, in line with their new found Spirit-boldness, refuse to accept the charge. It is their moral obligation before God to continue preaching Jesus. No further threats would deter them. The prosecuting group, at this juncture, is afraid to go any further because of the obvious popularity of these two men—due in large measure to the fresh memory of a cured forty-year-old man.

THE PRAYER OF THE APOSTLES 4:23–31

Peter and John make a report on the hearing to their friends. The group is moved to prayer. They address it to God as the creator of the universe. They cite the opening lines of psalm 2 showing how God, the sovereign king, protects his anointed one against any attack from lesser kings. In this they are establishing the Christian application of that psalm.

The earthly kings, Herod and Pontius Pilate, had acted against Jesus, the holy one of the Lord. Yet the creator had raised up his son. Now the earthly powers are in concert against the holy community of the Spirit. They beg for more Spirit-boldness, well aware that this opposition is clearly going to escalate.

The conclusion of their prayer is a kind of mini-Pentecost. The room is shaken. That minor earthquake is an answer from God, "Your prayers have been heard." Once again they are flooded with the Holy Spirit and they take note of the boldness with which they are able to speak the word of the Lord.

A point that must be learned from these stories is the insistence that conviction in proclaiming Jesus is a gift that comes from the inner working of the Spirit. The further away we stray from this fundamental affirmation of the founding Church, the more we tend to place the area of conviction in terms of logical correctness, mental clarity, and the persuasiveness of intellectual argument alone. There is no question that the daily strengthening of our intellectual ability to communicate the person of Jesus is very important. But without the boldness, that alone is a gift of the Spirit, our convictions will wither and unfortunately die out in the end. Intellectual effort must always be accompanied with the prayer for boldness. Hence we readily remember that grace and mystery surround our communications strivings—that all we own, we owe.

COMMON PROPERTY 4:32–37

It has already been noted that common life was a result of the pentecost event, and that sharing of property had been a typical act of the group. What must be made clear here, at the outset, is that this had always been voluntary. We are not sure how many of the first Christians practiced the kind of common life described in this passage. The most we can say is that enough examples of such communities exist that they constitute an important feature of early Church life and are thus worthy of comment.

The donation of Joseph Barnabas (v. 36) must have been considerable. It probably came in answer to a prayer, because the community is poor and would be the beneficiary of collections in the future. Hence the inclusion of his name is like the naming of an outstanding benefactor. His story is in bright contrast to the bleak tale of Ananias and Sapphira that will be told in chapter five.

The information in these passages is sparse. We would like to know the extent of these communities. Also, were the contributions shared only by members of the group, or were they shared with outsiders as well?

5 FIRST DEATHS AND THE GAMALIEL PRINCIPLE

FIRST DEATHS IN THE CHURCH 5:1—11

Now the first note of discord within the community is recorded. Ananias and Sapphira had sold their land and pretended to give the sum total to the communal treasury, where in reality they had concealed part of the money for themselves. Peter tells them they have been tempted by Satan to lie against the Holy Spirit. To sin against the Spirit is the greatest sin. It's the sort of thing that had made a traitor out of Judas.

Discipline demands that they be handed over to the Spirit for punishment. That comes very quickly, for with split-second timing, they die on the spot, the sound of their lie barely out of their mouths. The story is reminiscent of the Old Testament account of Achan. The city of Jericho had been captured with God's help, and at God's command all its treasure was to be destroyed and none taken by the troops.

"But Achan took goods that were under the ban (i.e. treasure) and the anger of the Lord flared up against the Israelites." (Joshua 7:1) Eventually, Achan was discovered and brought to trial. He admits he stowed away an expensive Shinar coat, 200 shekels of silver and a bar of gold weighing 50 shekels. The death sentence against him is immediate and swift. "And all Israel stoned him to death." (Joshua 7:25)

St. Paul tells of death coming suddenly on some people who had taken Communion unworthily. (I

Cor. 11:27-30) These mysterious deaths attributed to Satanic bonds, with divine revenge as a response, doubtless had caused a measure of terror in the early Church. In this, as well as in the Acts account, there is no talk of the possibility of salvation. The damning death is resolute and quick. However, Paul does speak in another place to the Corinthians about the real possibility of reform, conversion and salvation. "Get rid of the old yeast to make of yourselves fresh dough, unleavened loaves, as it were. Christ, our Passover, has been sacrificed. Let us celebrate the feast, not with the old yeast, that of corruption and wickedness, but with the unleavened bread of sincerity and truth." (I Cor. 5:6-8)

In the 11th verse, the community is called Church for the first time. It is a word based on the Hebrew term for a *called community,* in the sense that the congregation is not self-appointed, but the result of a vocation from God, a grace due to God's initiative. Our comments about the early Christians still praying at the Temple infer that the first community only gradually had come to see itself as a group radically new and separate from Judaism.

In the beginning, they feel they are still substantially of the house of Israel. They see themselves as having special synagogue status because they believe they are the true heirs of Abraham, while the others had corrupted the message. They are the "true believers." Eventually, however, they realize they are much more than a purified synagogue. They are indeed a new reality, a Church founded by Christ, graced by the Spirit and built on the foundation of the apostles.

SIGNS AND WONDERS 5:12–16

Once again the apostles return to Solomon's Portico. Their healing ministry expands, and now includes exorcism. They had failed at the latter during the historical ministry of Jesus because, as the Lord admonished them, they had neglected prayer and fasting. But now they heed Christ's message and understand that it is letting the power of the Spirit work through them. Non-believers are afraid to be seen with them, but this does not deter the sick from coming to the apostles for healing. In fact, the power of the healing Spirit had become so great that even the shadow of Peter is sufficient to mediate that consolation.

THE TWELVE ARE ARRESTED 5:17–42

Once again the Sanhedrin arrests not only Peter and John, but now all the apostles. The Mishna, a Hebrew legal code, provides that for a first offense, normally only an admonition is needed. But explicit punishment is deserved for subsequent misdeeds. Hence the apostles are now both admonished as well as put in jail. An angel comes and releases them, telling them to return to their ministry at the Temple. Peter will be released again from jail (Acts 12:10) but in that story the door simply opens, without benefit of angel.

It takes time for the authorities to realize their prisoners are free and back at work again. Police are sent to arrest them once more. The tactics are peaceful since they are afraid the people might riot. The high priest demands to know why they had broken the law again and preached Jesus. Peter gives the classical response of all highly principled and moral men. One is not to obey unjust laws of men when the higher law of God prevails.

Peter accuses them of hanging Jesus upon a tree, echoing a law from Deuteronomy which they had misused. "If a man guilty of a capital offense is put to death, and his corpse hung on a tree. . ." (Dt. 21:22) But God had raised Jesus from the dead so that Israel could repent and be forgiven its sins. Peter is basically telling the high priests of their guilt in killing an innocent man, but that forgiveness awaits them if they repent. In effect, Peter becomes the judge, and it is they who are standing on trial.

The Sanhedrin, understandably, is angered by Peter's stubborn position and role reversal that puts them on trial. But before tempers flare too high, Gamaliel speaks a more dispassionate word. He had been Paul's teacher (cf. Acts 22:3) and of the school of Hillel. He has favored a humane and literal interpretation of the law. While the party of Pharisees in Galilee have been known for their opposition to Jesus, those in Jerusalem have not. True, some reference is made to their hostility to Jesus in John's passion account, but the other writings show Jesus and the Jerusalem Pharisees had not had an adversary relationship.

The Gamaliel principle is a conciliatory and urbane view of divine providence—"If their purpose or activity is human in its origins, it will destroy itself. If on the other hand, it comes from God, you will not be able to destroy them without fighting God himself."—a kind of spiritual detente in which the opposition is let alone to either prove or hang himself.

To support his case, Gamaliel cited the examples of Theudas and Judas the Galilean. Presumably both men inspired revolutions which ended in their brutal demise and the dissipation of their followers. As cautionary tales they made a good argument. But as reflections of real history, they left something to be desired. Theudas led his revolt during the reign of Fadus in A.D. 44, years after Gamaliel was supposed to have given this talk. It was a fact that Theudas did fail and his forces dissolved.

More oddly yet, Gamaliel put the story of Theudas sequentially before that of Judas the Galilean who operated around A.D. 6, 38 years before Theudas. To further complicate matters, Judas' followers, the Zealots, did not disperse at his death, but actually held on until the destruction of the Temple in A.D. 70.

Today, it is not clear how these historical mix-ups came about in this passage. At any rate, the message of Gamaliel is valid and persuasive, regardless of the problems raised by the examples he uses.

The Sanhedrin accepts Gamaliel's advice. But they order the apostles scourged before letting them go, much as Pilate had scourged Jesus and then released him. Far from frustrating and discouraging the apostles, they are filled with joy at suffering the way Jesus had. They identify their wounds with those of the Savior and go back to their ministry with a new degree of fervor.

6 STEPHEN'S STORY

CHOOSING DEACONS 6:1–7

The growth of the community brings with it the usual administrative problems. We have already mentioned that there had been a good deal of poverty, and hence the need for alms and proper distribution. As it turns out, the widows of the Hellenists had been neglected, while those of the Hebrews had not. It is not absolutely clear who these Hebrews and Hellenists were.

The context of Acts to this point maintains that all the converts, so far, have been Jews. In this light, the probability is that the Hebrews had been Aramaic-speaking Jews and the Hellenists had been Greek-speaking Jews. In all likelihood, they had once lived in the diaspora—Greek-speaking territories—and had returned to make their home in Jerusalem.

The solution to the just distribution problem is the selection of seven men to act as deacons to perform the administrative service for the widows. They all have Greek names, but that does not mean necessarily they are all Hellenist Jews. At the head of the list is Stephen, a man full of faith and the Holy Spirit. They are ordained at a prayer service, and there is a ceremony of the laying on of hands. Though these men had been elected to do social service, they are thereafter depicted as preachers and defenders of the faith.

THE STORY OF STEPHEN 6:8–15

The action now converges on the synagogue of the Freedmen. The name comes from the fact that the members of this synagogue had been Jews freed from slavery. Stephen had been preaching at this place and had aroused the opposition of the congregation, especially the members from Cyrene and Alexandria. We must note again that even though the deacons had been primarily appointed for social service to the community, this had not prevented them from engaging in the preaching mission of the Church. Their roles had been clear, but not necessarily rigid.

Stephen and his adversaries debate one another. Stephen, however, is too powerful for them. As Luke stresses, Stephen speaks with "inspired wisdom." His opponents then set in motion a replay of the Passion of Christ. They allege that Stephen had said blasphemous things about God, had attacked the person and work of Moses and had undermined the value of Temple worship claiming that, deservedly, it would be destroyed by Jesus.

It is evident that the strategy against Stephen would be the same as that used in the trial of Jesus. Stephen would become the first martyr of the Church, and it is perhaps no accident that his ultimate witness would follow the precise path of Jesus himself. The use of false witnesses and the repetition of the accusations against Jesus has reminded us that the pursuit of the Gospel does involve the Way of the Cross. Pope John XXIII was often heard to say as he meditated on the Passion of Christ, "If they did it to him, they will do it to us. It is something that we can expect."

The accusation of blasphemy has been cited by all the Gospel writers in the case of Jesus. In a society where the consciousness of God was very central, and sacred matters held a high priority in the life of the people, an act of blasphemy was an especially serious matter. It was not only a religious sin, but a "secular" crime deserving of criminal punishment. Of all the criticisms they could have leveled against Stephen, this was the most inflammatory. All of chapter seven will be devoted to the story of Stephen's defense and martyrdom.

7 THE FACE OF AN ANGEL

STEPHEN'S DISCOURSE 7:1-53

Court speeches at this time normally did not dwell on the defense of self so much as the cause in question. Stephen was anxious to use the court as a platform for the defense of the Gospel of Jesus and the meaning of the new Church. The special importance of his speech was that it signaled the formal break of Christianity with Judaism. From this time onward the Church explicitly saw itself as a new manifestation of God's will in the world. This consciousness grew continuously and assumed a definite reality at the destruction of the Temple.

The substance of Stephen's presentation was the history of Israel from Abraham to Solomon. He used the story to show how Israel was opposed to Jesus, in the sense that Israel had a long record of hostility to the prophets and yielded to the temptations to idolatry. As they had stoned the prophets, so now they crucified Jesus. As they had worshiped the golden calf, and the idol Moloch, so now they made the Temple a setting for self-worship and not a locale for adoring the living God.

The story begins with Abraham, a nomad, whom God promises a special land in which to settle and dwell. But in fact, when Abraham had arrived in the promised land, God had not given him the property at all. Instead God had assured him that at some future date his descendants would have the land. Stephen stresses that it was the obedience of Abraham that eventually sets the fulfillment of this promise in motion.

The narrative moves to the story of the brothers of Joseph who had been jealous of him and thus blinded to God's will for his future. In this their opposition is contrasted to the obedience of Abraham. The persecution of Joseph is a forecast of the sufferings that would be inflicted on Jesus. God, however, had disregarded the resistance of the brothers and had proceeded to realize his purposes in Joseph. The parallels are clear in the minds of the judges of the court. The rejected Joseph exemplifies their attitude both toward Jesus and the Church that stands for his message.

Stephen favors circumcision as a longstanding and revered sign of man's covenant with God. As we will see later, Paul considers circumcision in a different light when encountering the non-circumcision culture of the gentiles. This question will be debated and settled at a solemn meeting of the Church in Jerusalem (cf. chapter 15). The Joseph story proceeds according to the familiar pattern. In the heat of his discourse, Stephen misplaces the tomb of Abraham at Sichem instead of Mamre (v. 15). "Abraham buried his wife Sarah in the cave on the plot of the field of Machpelah, facing Mamre. . . . There Abraham was buried with his wife Sarah." (Genesis 23:19; 49:31)

Next Stephen turns to the story of Moses. Some years after Joseph's rule in Egypt there arose a pharaoh who had resented the Jewish presence in his land and had set out to persecute and exploit them. God touches the conscience of Moses to arouse the people and persuade them to resist this tyranny. Moses also is portrayed as an image of Jesus, because he is both the favored one of God and a true executive of the divine will as well as a savior of the people.

Stephen recounts the classical details of the Moses story: (1) his slaying of the cruel Egyptian foreman, (2) his flight to Midian where he marries and fathers two sons, (3) his encounter at the burning bush where he hears the holy name of God and receives his commission to save his people, (4) the crossing of the Red Sea and the pilgrimage to Sinai, (5) Aaron and the golden calf, (6) The

Tent of Testimony (basically a portable Temple).

Stephen gears the Moses story to his own purposes. In citing Moses' prediction that God "will raise up . . . a prophet like me" (v. 37) Stephen is clearly saying that Jesus is that prophet. His emphasis on the idolatry of the golden calf and of Moloch (v. 40,43) is to remind them that their Temple worship today is still an idolatry for they forget the living God and celebrate simply the works of their own hands.

He carries his argument against the Temple further by his reference to the Tent of Testimony. This was a portable temple which they carried with them during their nomadic days. It was a center of worship for the traveling community. Often the cloud-glory of God's presence would settle upon the tent and thus renew God's faithful covenant with his people. As the people moved "under God's Temple of the cosmos" the Tent of Testimony went with them. In this way God was seen as the divine shepherd leading his people through their many wanderings, just as the human shepherds led the sheep.

When the people finally settle in the Promised Land, at last receiving the gift that had been promised to Abraham, they ask Solomon to build a Temple. Stephen dismisses the usual reverence for the Temple and immediately points out that the Most High does not live in houses built by the hands of man. (v. 47) This expression about the hands of man is a common put-down for idols. Stephen reminds them that no less an authority than Isaiah states that heaven is God's throne and the earth his footstool. What kind of house could contain God? (Isaiah 66:1-2)

It must be understood here that Stephen is

engaging in special pleading. Therefore, he is emphasizing only the darker pages in the history of Israel, namely, the continuing thread of their stubborn resistance to God's will, which appears again in their treatment of Jesus and the Church as new and decisive manifestations of God's hope for man. Like a lawyer in arguing a case, he is using selective perception to make the point.

The reason for making this observation about Stephen is that it is equally clear that he is not against the Temple, but only against a Temple that is no longer a "Tent of Meeting." It has lost the free spirit and charismatic quality which had characterized the days of the Exodus, the pilgrimage to Sinai, and the nomadic freedom of the time of the judges. His argument really is that the Temple could be a true meeting-ground with God, but that it is no longer so. They prize the house of the Lord—not the Lord of the house.

A second element of selective perception that Stephen uses effectively in his case is to portray Israel as meeting God only outside the confines of the Promised Land. It is in exile and in wandering that the people really know their Lord. He seems to imply that once they had settled in Jerusalem and had encased God in a Temple, their effective union with the Lord begins to disappear.

This theme is almost like a preface to the remainder of Acts, for in ever-widening circles, the story of the new Church moves beyond Jerusalem to the ends of the earth. The gradual overshadowing of Jerusalem by numerous new missions of the Church symbolizes both the growing opposition of Judaism and Christianity at that early priod and, by implication, that the real covenant community is not tied to one land—much less to a Temple.

Stephen concludes his argument with an intense criticism of his accusers. Like Peter putting the Sanhedrin on trial, Stephen stands in judgment on these resisters of the Holy Spirit. He is well aware that prophets like himself are always brutalized and murdered. He reminds his listeners of this traditional response, implies that they will no doubt follow the same route, and appears ready to be the new victim in a long line of martyrs. (His reference to the Law being mediated by angels was an expression of the sacred character of the Law, something his persecutors seem to have forgotten.)

STEPHEN DIES 7:54–8:1a

Stephen is correct in his estimation that his listeners had reached the classical murderous position toward one so outspokenly judgmental of their consciences. The young deacon looks away from their faces and up to the heavens where he sees a vision of Jesus under the title "Son of Man." This is an expression which Jesus had used about himself seventy times in the Gospels. It had had a double meaning, based on its use in Ezechiel and Daniel.

Ezechiel frequently employed the term, Son of Man, to refer to the contrast between man and God. Like Ash Wednesday, "Remember man, that you are dust . . ." Daniel spoke of a Son of Man that would be a savior and messiah, establishing God's rule on the earth. Jesus re-adapted Ezechiel's usage and affirmed himself as a real man, like all humans, except he was without sin. His divinity was not in question here, just that the emphasis of the expression was on his humanity.

It is obvious that Daniel's use of the term applies to Jesus' role as messiah and savior. Stephen's use of the Son of Man title for Jesus is the only New Testament example of this outside the Gospels.

The violence and unrestrained character of this scene suggest that we are not dealing here with a formal trial. It seems a lot more like a lynching. No formalities. No sentencing. Just a wild rush of angry people determined to rid themselves of this sting to their consciences. Like Jesus, he is taken outside the city walls for the execution.

The mob place their outer garments at the feet of Saul, giving us our first introduction to Paul. Paul had been a student of Gamaliel (Acts 22:3), but he broke from his master's principle and had planned a fanatic repression of these Christians. Deuteronomy 17:7 tells what the order of stoning shall be: "At the execution, the witnesses are to be the first to raise their hands against him; afterward all the people are to join in." Then this man with the face "of an angel" (Acts 6:15) kneels and places his spirit in the hands of the Lord and forgives his enemies.

And Saul agrees to the murder of Stephen.

8 TERROR IN THE CHURCH

THE CHURCH IS TERRORIZED 8:1b–3

The murder of Stephen occasions terrorism against the Church in Jerusalem. Many flee to Samaria, with the positive result that the Gospel is now being heard beyond the confines of Jerusalem. Missionary expansion begins. It is noted that Saul, with the typical ruthlessness of a zealot, had raided the homes of Christians and had dragged them off to prison. The devout men who bury Stephen belong to the age-old tradition of respectful burying the abandoned dead as celebrated in the book of Tobit. "One of my people who had died and been thrown outside the walls of Niniveh, I would bury him." (Tobit 1:17)

THE STORY OF PHILIP IN SAMARIA 8:4–25

Just as nothing is said about Stephen's social-service mission as a deacon, but rather his preaching and witnessing in Jerusalem, so now deacon Philip's mission preaching to Samaria is all that is mentioned. He preaches Christ and performs exorcisms and many healings. Many are converted and baptized in the name of Jesus. The news is brought to Jerusalem, and Peter and John are sent up to confirm the new group in the Holy Spirit. One special interpretation of the coming of the apostles was to show that a recognizable institutional Church was in the process of formation and this was best dramatized by direct contact with the apostles.

It must be admitted the passage presents some difficulty. The converts had been baptized in the name of Jesus yet had not received the Holy Spirit (v. 15). It may mean that the signs of the Holy Spirit's presence, which had taken so many visible manifestations since Pentecost, were not yet apparent in these new members. Another suggested meaning is that Luke wishes to show that the normal mediator of the Spirit is the institutional Church, as represented by the apostles in this story.

The figure of Simon Magus was worked in and out of this narrative. He was a prominent self-promoter, calling himself a "great person." He sold his audiences on this line and was regarded by them as the so-called "power of the great God."

He created a problem for the missionaries, since he, along with many gentile magicians, roamed the countryside preaching and healing and doing marvels. The Christian missionaries had to make sure they were not confused with magicians. One thing was apparent, that the Christian wonder-workers surpassed the magicians quite handily.

Simon is astonished by the superiority of the Christian wonder-workers, particularly the ability of the baptized to speak in tongues and to prophesy. Simon offers to pay for the secret of performing such impressive wonders. His act is the origin of the word *simony*, which in the Middle Ages will refer to the purchase of ecclesiastical offices, and not the buying of spiritual expertise.

Peter tells the magician that this is not a trick that can be sold but rather a spiritual act resulting from a gift of God. He advises Simon to get rid of his materialistic views and open himself to the Spirit. Peter lets the magician off comparatively easily. Medieval sanctions against simony will be far more severe. Simon has the good grace to ask Peter to pray that the Lord will not let him slide into the "bitterness and chains of sin." (v. 23)

CONVERTING AN ETHIOPIAN 8:26–40

The scene switches abruptly to the Gaza road which runs along the Mediterranean coast down towards Egypt. Philip is prompted to go there by an angel. He finds an Ethiopian who is returning from a pilgrimage to Jerusalem where he has been firming up his status as a candidate for conversion to Judaism. He is meditating on the 53rd chapter of Isaiah in which the prophet describes the suffering that comes to the good man the poem calls "the servant."

The Spirit prompts Philip to break in on the Ethiopian's reverie. He finds out the Ethiopian is an official of *the* Candace, the queen, of Ethiopia. Candace is not a proper name, but a title for a queen, like "pharaoh" is the title of a king. Philip notes that the official is reading aloud from Isaiah. Our age of silent readers must remember there was a time when oral reading was the norm, and lip reading was not considered the retrograde behavior it is today—in private or for study.

The text is about the suffering servant. Philip asks the Ethiopian if he knows the meaning of what he reads. The official replies that he needs to have someone explain this passage to him. Thereupon, Philip takes the passage and interprets it in terms of Jesus and proceeds to give his friend an evangelical instruction. Philip is unusually effective, for very soon, as they are passing a pool, the Ethiopian asks to be baptized. Philip promptly complies, and his friend goes joyfully on his way.

Meanwhile, in some miraculous fashion, Philip is transported from Gaza over to Azotus and Caesarea where he continues his missionary preaching. We shall hear from Philip again after he marries and breeds four unmarried daughters and settles down in Caesarea, where he welcomes the veteran missionary Paul to his home. (Acts 21:8)

9 *VESSEL OF THE SPIRIT*

SAUL'S CONVERSION 9:1–19a

This is the first of three accounts in the Acts about the conversion of Saul into Paul, the apostle to the gentiles. (See also 22:1-16 and 26:9-18). The accounts agree in substance, while differing in detail. There is even a fourth narrative by Paul in his letter to the Galatians 1:11-26. The conversion stories in Acts seem to come at pivotal moments in the growth of the Church.

The conversion account in chapter nine dwells on the theme of bringing the Gospel to the gentiles. The story of converting Cornelius, the first gentile, comes immediately afterwards. The second conversion narrative in chapter 22 ties up with the efforts of the Church to disengage itself from its Jewish background. The third story in chapter 26 tells the story in the light of Saul's appeal to Caesar and thus the movement of the Church "to the ends of the earth."

The story opens with Saul and his companions traveling to Damascus with extradition papers, intent on arresting Christians and bringing them "bound" back to Jerusalem. There has been some discussion as to how the high priest would have such legal powers as to send "sacral policemen" into a foreign country to round up undesirable religious enemies. The first book of Machabees, 15:21, does say that Rome endows the high priest with power to pursue fugitives with the power of extradition. At any rate, Saul somehow receives the proper papers to raid Christian homes in Damascus.

Along the way, Saul is overwhelmed by a religious experience that totally changes his life. The details of blinding light, shuddering awe and challenging questioning are similar to other experiences in the Old Testament. Moses finds the light in the burning bush, is penetrated with awe on the holy ground and receives the challenge to save his people. Isaiah gazes into the light of the glory of God surrounded by the seraphim (literally the fire-angels), is awed by the sense of his own sinfulness before such holiness and accepts from God the challenge to purify the people. (Cf. Isaiah 6)

Ezechiel, by the river Chobar in Babylon, sees the light in terms of whirling suns. In awe, he falls to the ground before the glory and hears the charge from God that he must convert the people from their sinfully rebellious ways. (Ezechiel 1-2) Hence the experience of Saul is in the classical line of biblical religious experiences, only in his case the stakes are nothing less than worldwide.

It is Jesus himself who speaks to Saul, rebuking him for persecuting him in his brethren. This recalls the sermon of Jesus in Matthew 25, where he illustrates that whatever is done to the least of the brethren is done to him. Now Saul is to go into the city and await further instructions. His companions hear the voice but see nothing, whereas in the other two accounts they seem to see a light, but not hear anything.

Because Saul is blind, his friends must lead him to the house of Judas on Straight Street in Damascus. Meanwhile, Jesus appears in a vision to Ananias and tells him to go to Judas' house and cure the blindness of Saul of Tarsus. Ananias argues with Christ that this man is an enemy of Christians and is commissioned to persecute them. In passing, it should be noted that this argumentative posture toward the Lord is a form of prayer practically unknown among us these days. Yet biblical people thought it natural in their conversations with the Lord to argue and struggle with him. Jacob's wrestling with the Lord and Job's loud complaints to God are two vivid examples of this kind of praying.

Jesus tells Ananias that Saul is now a chosen instrument, a "vessel of election" divinely appointed to carry the holy name to the gentiles, to kings and to Israel. Saul would indeed fulfill each of these missions as he bore the Word to the gentiles, spoke it bravely in the sight of kings and argued it forcefully with the leaders of Israel.

Ananias complies with the Lord's will, goes to see Saul and tells him that Jesus wishes him to regain his sight and receive the Holy Spirit. He baptizes Saul, who thereupon recovers his sight and is filled with the Spirit. As always, the Acts dwell on the central importance of the presence and power of the Spirit. This is a reminder of the source of the energy of the Church, the origin of the drive that moves missionaries to bring Jesus to the ends of the earth, the fountain from which comes the courage to face any kind of threat or pain.

Saul will be a superb vessel of the Spirit, making exhausting journeys, announcing Jesus with boldness and absorbing enough pain—in terms of stonings, scourgings and humiliations—for a hundred missionaries in ten lifetimes. The message is simple; namely, to have a soul that is open and welcoming to the Spirit. The results are evident. The simplicity is not simplistic. Certainly, many obstacles bar people from becoming a child again, as Jesus advised, in order to await the Spirit. Our complex age appears to forbid so straightforward an approach. The contemplation of Acts should stir the readers to reconsider their own personal flexibility and allow a door to be open to the Spirit's creative coming.

SAUL'S EXPERIENCES IN DAMASCUS AND JERUSALEM 9:19b–30

The gift of the Spirit moves the receiver to testimony. Saul, with all the vigor he once reserved against Christians, now uses his testimony for Christ. He goes to the synagogues and astonishes them all by proclaiming that Jesus is son of God and Messiah. They are amazed that one who so recently had hated Christ now speaks so zealously and lovingly in his behalf.

They find it difficult to argue with him because his native brilliance plus his training as a Pharisee has equipped him to be a powerful advocate of his cause. Gradually, he generates a murderous opposition from some members of the local synagogue. So severe is the threat that he has to escape the city at night, while hiding in a basket that is lowered down the city wall.

In Galatians 1:17 Paul says that he spent three years in the Arabian desert after his conversion, presumably absorbing the impact of what happened to him and strengthening his soul for the great missionary years ahead. Luke omits this story here in the Acts, though most likely it would fit after the escape from Damascus.

Next Saul goes to Jerusalem to get in contact with the apostles. It is hard for them to believe he is sincere when they can remember how many of their own had been terrorized by him. Perhaps some are still in prison due to his fanatical efforts. A man named Barnabas intercedes for him with the apostles, telling them the story of his conversion, his courageous preaching at Damascus and subsequent escape.

He finds acceptance with the disciples and then goes about Jerusalem preaching the Word with *boldness*. Over and over again the Acts mention the boldness, the courage with which the disciples proclaim the Lord. We have already dwelt on this gift of the Spirit earlier, but it is worth repeating here

as does the Acts. Critics of Christianity love to
dwell not only on the lack of Christian practice but
also on the noticeable absence of compelling conviction on the part of those appointed to proclaim
the Word.

It may be a persuasive message in its logical pattern, but it doesn't seem true as it falls from the
lips of the heralds. They lack the gift of boldness
from the Spirit. It is a gift that must be prayed for
and not just studied over.

As in the case of Stephen, Saul brings the message to the Hellenists. Just as Stephen's boldness
had been too much for them, so is Saul's. They
promptly plan to kill him. His friends, however,
spirit him away to Caesarea from which city he
went to his home at Tarsus.

PETER GOES TO LYDDA AND JOPPA 9:31–43

The Church begins to grow in Galilee and
Samaria. Luke says they are enjoying peace. This
seems odd in the light of the previous stories, unless
Luke might mean an inner peace that knows Christ
will triumph over all opposition. They enjoy the
"comfort" of the Holy Spirit. Those who know the
Spirit frequently testify to the consolation that
comes from his presence. The liturgy of Pentecost
makes many allusions to the comforting presence,
the "balm of the soul" that characterizes an abiding work of the Spirit.

The growth of converts is not attributed to the
skill, energy and eloquence of the missionaries, but
rather to the Spirit who is the ultimate awakener of
the hearts of men through the missionaries, his in-
struments.

The attention returns to Peter and his evangelical travels. He comes to Lydda, a town about

25 miles south of Jerusalem and inland from the
coastal town of Joppa, to which he will journey
next. He visits Aeneas, telling him to get up and
make his bed, for Jesus has healed him. The healing sign is a Gospel, a good news, that draws many
to accept Christ. Again this emphasis on healing
teaches that Christ does not want people to be sick
or to suffer. His good news is that he and his disciples are come to heal the broken-hearted and
broken-bodied. The ministry of healing in the apostolic Church is a normal and daily occurrence.
And it certainly was good-news Gospel.

Next Peter goes to Joppa and visits the widow
Tabitha, which in Greek is Dorcas, meaning "Ga-
zelle". She is a widow. As we have seen, widows are
normally poor and, therefore, in need of regular
charity. Dorcas had been known for her own kind-
ness and charity during her life, hence her death is
more than ordinarily mourned.

Peter is asked to come. He finds the widows of
the town deeply grieved. They show him clothes
that Dorcas had made for them. Peter asks them
to leave. He prays and then commands her to rise.
Her raising from the dead occasions a widespread
growth of belief in the Lord. Peter stays some days
in Joppa with a tanner named Simon.

10 THE STORY OF CORNELIUS

BRINGING CHRIST TO THE GENTILES 10:1–48

The Spirit moves the Church to take seriously
the project of bringing Christ to the gentile world.
It is difficult for us, so many centuries later, to realize this was not an obvious conclusion for the first

Christians. It is evident to us that the message of Jesus should be available to all people. In the beginning this wasn't clear at all.

The first Christians were Jews possessing the Hebrew mind set that God's covenant was only meant for Jews. It is true that some converts were made from the gentiles, but this was exceptional. The rules for acceptance were severe enough to discourage growth of the practice. Along with this religious exclusivism went a life style that set apart the people both in theological outlook, worship practices, dietary laws and the custom of circumcision.

This was a cultural corral that set the Jewish people apart and implied their superiority to the gentiles who were somewhat viewed as an "unclean race." To become a Christian did not mean leaving Judaism; it meant becoming a perfect Jew, at last completely fulfilling the hope of the law. Conversion to Christianity bore no ecumenical or universal meaning at first. The details of Jewish religion, cultural life and exclusivist mind set remained.

What Christianity brought, they thought, was the triumph of the prophets' hopes, a community-wide experience of God's Spirit, healing and hope for the sick and poor, exorcism for the possessed and resurrection from the dead. The idea that these marvels could and should be available also to the gentiles needed a special intervention of the Spirit to cause the broadening of outlook.

The Gospels show there was some interest in religious contact with the gentiles as evidenced in the stories of the Syro-Phoenician woman and the devout centurion. The conversion of St. Paul, Philip's mission to Samaria and experience with the Ethiopian, the martyrdom of Stephen and the growing persecution of Christians by Judaism set the scene for a new consciousness.

Left to themselves the early Jewish Christians might have kept the Christ experience within their group. The Spirit came, in the light of the events mentioned above, and shook them from their fixed positions so that they inaugurated a universal mission to all nations and peoples. These comments are not meant to put down the first Christians, for, like them, we all live within the blindness of our own cultural limitations. We must always be grateful that the Spirit generously entered our lives and broke the mold of our fixed views. The Cornelius story taught us that the Holy Spirit will constantly surprise us into new horizons.

The Cornelius narrative opens with the account of his work and a vision. He lives in Caesarea, a rich seacoast city near Mt. Carmel. Herod the Great had built the city and had named it after Caesar Augustus. Cornelius is a Roman centurion of the Italian cohort. A centurion is in charge of one hundred soldiers. A cohort is a division of six hundred troops. Acts notes the piety of Cornelius who is known for both his public charity and personal prayer life.

A certain number of gentiles had acquired an interest in Judaism. They embraced the notion of the one God, favored biblical morality and practiced some of the details of the Mosaic Law. They didn't try to join the Jewish religion, but they were fascinated by it and drawn to its ideals. The New Testament shows that some of the military, during their tour of duty in Palestine, were especially attracted.

A comparison from today is the current enchantment of our young with eastern religions. There is a fascination with meditation techniques, dietary customs such as vegetarianism and the peaceful philosophy of eastern sages.

Cornelius adopts the prayer hours of the pious Jew. It is on one of these occasions that an angel appears to him and tells him that his prayers and generosity deserve a reward from the Lord. He should send for a man called Peter. So Cornelius dispatches some messengers to bring Peter to Caesarea.

Meanwhile, Peter also has a vision in which a feast is laid before him. The problem is that the meat was "unclean," forbidden by the dietary laws of Judaism. Leviticus 11:2-23 gives a long and intriguing list of forbidden meats: ham, camel, seagull, owl, stork, bat (!) and many others. Most of us are familiar with the taboo against pig meat. We are not told what was on that celestial table, but Peter clearly would not touch taboo foods. Peter echoes the words of Ezechiel, "I have never eaten anything unclean." (Ez. 5:14)

God tells Peter to eat, for he has purified all. The lesson is that if there is no unclean food, then there will not be "unclean" people, namely gentiles. The division of Jew and non-Jew is to be dissolved. The Spirit unites all people in Christ. As Paul writes later to the Ephesian gentiles, "You are no longer strangers, but fellow citizens with the saints and members of the household of God." The removal of the religious prejudicial taboo against certain foods symbolizes the need for the removal of the religious prejudicial taboo against gentiles.

The servants of Cornelius bring Peter the invitation to visit him. When Peter arrives, Cornelius greets him with a profound bow normally reserved for religious adoration. Peter is embarrassed and reminds Cornelius that he is only a man. He also conveys an additional shyness, for he has never before entered the house of a gentile—much the same as prejudice has kept various racial and ethnic groups in our country from ever entering each others' homes.

Peter states that it took a vision from God to shake him from his life-long conviction that a gentile is ritually unclean—a religious lesson that should not be lost on us who may have our own black list of ritually unclean (socially unacceptable) people. Cornelius welcomes Peter and tells him the story of his own vision.

Then Peter replies with the last of his great sermons in the Acts. He follows the established pattern of a conversion to Christ talk as found in Acts. He proclaims the great events of Christ's life, his baptism, his ministry in Galilee with its miracles, his journey to Jerusalem and the parables, his passion, resurrection and exaltation. Peter calls for faith in Jesus.

That faith already appears in the household of Cornelius, for even as Peter speaks the Holy Spirit takes hold of his new listeners. The descent of the Spirit in the house of Cornelius has been called the "Gentile Pentecost." The event surprises the "circumcised," that is, the Jewish Christians who are accompanying Peter on this visit. Their psychology had already been wrenched by standing inside the home of a gentile. Now they are to think the unthinkable: the Holy Spirit is just as available to gentiles as he is to them. They witness the gentiles speaking in tongues and praising God.

Peter, commenting on this visible manifestation of the Spirit, calls for the baptism of Cornelius and his household. As Jesus once said to Nicodemus, "Don't be surprised . . . The wind (Spirit) breathes where he wills." (John 3:8) Nor should we be surprised that the Spirit comes upon these people prior to their sacramental Baptism. God prepared their hearts and the sacrament celebrated and confirmed their faith and dedication to Christ and their membership in the Church.

11 *MISSION TO ANTIOCH*

THE CIRCUMCISION ADVOCATES 11:1–18

It didn't take long for the news about the Cornelius event to reach the Jewish Christian communities. Their puzzled and angry reaction was sincere and understandable, given their cultural and religious heritage and mind set. We have already attempted to offer some insight into the psychology of the original converts to Christ. They are called here the "circumcision party," because of the centrality of this ritual as a sign of being a covenant person. It stood as a visible consecration of those who were children of Abraham.

They demand an explanation from Peter. How could he have been so liberal? What could have entered his mind to prompt him to fraternize with gentiles? How could he have dared to step inside a gentile's home? Worse yet, what would have moved him to actually baptize gentiles? These must be seen as honest questions, agonizingly put, and not self-righteous or petty quarreling over what happened. Given the limitations imposed on them by their education, culture and centuries of tradition, they would have been remiss in their consciences not to have raised these serious challenges.

Peter's reply is worthy of a modern communications expert. Carefully, he takes them through each stage of the development. He wants them to know all the facts, so they can judge for themselves, and get some feel for this extraordinary experience and the new consciousness that the infant Church must expand toward. Again, central to his exposition, is the insistence of the Holy Spirit's role in providing the insight that welcomes this new possibility.

If the Spirit had not urged this, if it had not been of God, then it could not have happened. Peter clearly sees it as a manifestation of the Spirit's will. He testifies to the gift of the Spirit appearing in these new believers in Jesus and claims that it would be dishonest for him to deny it. What is so evidently of God requires humble and joyous acceptance. The text reports that the circumcision party believes Peter and accepts this revolutionary step.

However, the subsequent history of the New Testament Church shows that this problem would continue to bedevil the community of believers. A new idea is rarely accepted with calm and prompt satisfaction. Chapter 15 of Acts demonstrates that the acceptance of this principle required solemn promulgation, and Paul would find himself arguing many times for the right of gentiles to embrace Jesus without accepting Jewish religio-cultural practices in the area of circumcision and diet.

THE ANTIOCH MISSION 11:19–30

Persecutions produce refugees. The martyrdom of Stephen had triggered a wave of terror, sending many Christians off to safer territories. Many had fled to Antioch, the provincial capitol of Syria and third largest city of the Roman empire. Noted for its large colony of Jews, it had been an obvious mecca for Jewish Christian evangelists.

The awakening consciousness of the need to bring the Gospel to the gentiles creates a need for establishing a mission to the Greek population in Antioch. Luke describes the considerable success of this mission with an Old Testament expression that "the hand of the Lord was with them." This vision of the centrality of the Lord's power is never lost in describing the work of the preachers of the Word. If no other lesson is learned from pondering the Bible's description of the Church's growth, this one of the overriding presence of the Spirit must be assimilated. Human effort and trial are never ignored, but the divine origin of the Church's expansion is never forgotten.

Luke writes that the number of converts had been so numerous that a special delegate from Jerusalem is sent to supervise the development. Barnabas acts as a liaison between Jerusalem and the new community in Antioch. His religious "job description" is emphasized, for he is a man full of the Spirit and faith. Given the context, this is a self-evident characterization. Yet, something may be learned by clearly designating this as a radical requirement for ministers of the Word. The human tendency, when gripped by the demands of the "nitty-gritty" of life is to assume the faith need, and then gradually forget it. Luke makes sure we don't forget.

Barnabas decides that the gentile mission at Antioch deserves the powerful presence of a man like Saul. He travels to Tarsus and convinces him to join the Antioch efforts. It is there that the followers of Jesus first receive the name Christians.

Some questions remain unresolved here. What were the relations between the Jewish and gentile Christians? Was their spirit and practice ecumenical? Did they visit each other's homes? Did they pray together? How were their charitable funds dispersed? Did they have Breaking of the Bread in common? Were the Jewish Christians uneasy about their gentile brethren?

We have some clues that all the Jewish Christians at Antioch were not convinced about the new approach of having gentile Christians get by without circumcision, at least. Some Jewish Christians from Antioch raised the circumcision protest at the Jerusalem gathering described in Acts 15. Galatians 2 records that some Jewish Christians in Antioch stopped dining with their gentile counterparts after they met with emissaries from James. Since, however, very little was written about their general relations in Antioch, we may be able to rest with the old proverb that "no news is good news." Most likely, their relations were amiable in large part.

After Barnabas and Saul had been working a year in Antioch, alarming news comes from a visiting prophet, Agabus. The word "prophet" here is used in the sense Paul writes of in I Corinthians 12; namely, a person gifted by the Spirit to preach Jesus. Technically, this gift is called a *charism* and thus the preacher is a charismatic person.

Agabus tells the community that a worldwide famine is imminent. Historically, this did not happen, though there was a local famine in Palestine during the reign of Claudius. The best wager on a date is A.D. 46. The Christians at Antioch already are sympathetic to their persecuted brethren in Jerusalem and surrounding territory. The prospect of a famine quickens their generosity even more, and Saul and Barnabas are dispatched with a sizable relief fund for the beleaguered community.

12 PETER IN CHAINS

HEROD PERSECUTES THE CHURCH 12:1—25

The stories of the reigns of terror against the first Christians assumed a climax in the official attack of Herod Agrippa, grandson of Herod the Great. Herod Agrippa had been involved in imperial affairs since he was a young man. He had had firsthand experiences of the resistance of the Jews against the emperor worship that had been insisted on by Caligula.

This emperor was bent on having a gigantic statue of himself erected in the Temple. He ordered his representative, Petronius, to see that it was done. Petronius refused. Caligula ordered him to commit suicide. Fortunately for Petronius, the emperor was assassinated and succeeded by the milder Claudius who was elected by the Roman army.

Herod supported Claudius, and for his loyalty was given charge of Judea and Samaria. He admired the religious courage of the Jews in the face of imperial ruthlessness. He was especially considerate of the Pharisees and impressed with the religious courage they inspired in their people. This turned out to be bad luck for the emerging Christian community. Herod would naturally share the hostility of the Pharisees to the upstart group. Moreover, like most leaders, he wanted no major disturbing influences in his province and so lent the weight of government forces against the Christians.

Seeing this from his point of view is small comfort for the Christians and not meant to be a whitewash of his motives. Enlightened rulers have better ways of handling internal problems. On the definitely negative side, he employed the typical pogrom tactics that all authoritarian rulers readily use, especially when suppressing religious and ideological opposition. He executed James, the son of Zebedee, captured Peter and imprisoned him in anticipation of a death trial.

This great sorrow for the Church took place in the days of the Unleavened Bread, another name for the Passover, the very time in which Jesus our Savior also met his passion and death. It may be useful here to comment on the origin of the title Unleavened Bread and its association with Passover.

Pagan peoples had always associated their worship with the events of nature. They celebrated the harvests, the births of flocks and the arrivals of the new moon with religious rites. The early Jews were familiar with the pagan religious practices. The genius of Israel was to transform these nature rituals into historical rites celebrating the mighty works which God had performed for them.

The pagans already had Unleavened Bread and Passover festivals before the Jews came to Palestine. The Unleavened Bread ritual was a farmers' festival giving thanks and taking joy for the successful barley harvest. The Passover was a religious ceremony illustrating similar sentiments at the birth of a new flock of spring lambs.

Israel, too, would worry through its agricultural output and the fertility of its animals. But Israel looked beyond the abundance of nature to the grace of God, who not only assured fertility and fecundity, but who also entered into the story of their lives. How could they ever forget the God of the Exodus and Sinai? They knew he favored the fields that grain might flourish and touched the ewes that new lambs would be born. They were even more grateful that he felt their humiliation in Egypt and saved them from potential genocide.

That was an historical moment they must forever cherish. Hence, they combined the earthly simplicity of nature rites with the grandeur of their faith memory and attached the new meanings to the feast of the Unleavened Bread and Passover. The ensuing centuries saw these simple celebrations evolve into stately rites with many additional meanings derived from continuing graces from God. The particular expression Unleavened Bread meant that, with the arrival of new grain, the old yeast was thrown away. Bread without leaven was eaten during the feast. New leaven was being created just as a new harvest was on their threshold. Paul would take the image of old leaven as a sign of sin which can be purged, so that a new life in Christ could begin with the Unleavened Bread-life of sincerity and truth.

To return to the story, Peter is imprisoned. The tightest security is required, so four sets of four guards each watch him round the clock. Fervent prayer groups storm heaven for his release. Peter is in chains. But when God wills freedom for his beloved, nothing will hold him back. An angel comes to the prison, touches the side of Peter, wakes him up. The chains fall off; Peter dresses and walks out a free man. It happens so suddenly and mysteriously that even he thought it must be a dream. But it is no dream. He is free and he realizes that it is the Lord himself who has liberated him.

It is popular for our scientific minds to think we are the only ones who have the right to be skeptical and doubting. We know the facts and do not accept such stories. It is both humbling and refreshing to note that our Christian forebears in the very heart of the apostolic Church were quite as capable of plain doubt. Peter arrives at Mary's house and tries to get in.

The guard in the middle of the night is a woman, Rhoda, which may show they had their own form of women's lib. She hears him but can't believe her ears. She wakes the household and tells them the story. And as believers have so often been told, they tell her, "You are mad." Peter's persistent knocking and their subsequent discovery discloses the truth. He tells them about the Lord's grace. They rejoice and give thanks.

Herod soon hears about the escape. He examines the guards and orders them executed. This cruel procedure had been common enough in early penal code. Guards in death row are responsible for their prisoner, even to the point of their own deaths if they fail to keep the prisoner from escaping.

The chapter ends with Herod's own grisly demise. He had been feuding with the Tyrians and Sidonians. It is not clear what the issue had been. Tyre and Sidon had depended on Herod for their food supply, hence they could not have afforded a long dispute. They negotiate with Blastus, the king's deputy, and arrange peace terms.

On the settlement day, Herod is attending a public spectacle in honor of Caesar. Luke says he is splendidly dressed and the people acclaim him as a

God. This same story is confirmed in the writings
of Josephus, an ancient historian:

"Herod's robes were woven completely of silver
so that its texture was indeed marvelous. The silver, illuminated by the first rays of the sun, was
wondrously radiant, and by its glitter it inspired
fear and awe in those who gazed upon it. His flat-
terers raised their voices from all directions—
though hardly for his good—addressing him as a
God." (Antiquities 19:8,2)

Luke then describes an angel of the Lord striking
him down. He does not give God the glory. Worms
eat at him and he dies. Josephus is no less dra-
matic:

"Herod looked up and saw an owl perched on a
rope over his head. He recognized it as a harbinger
of woes. He felt a stab of pain in his heart. He was
gripped in his stomach by an ache that was felt everywhere at once. Exhausted by the pain in his
abdomen after five straight days, he departed this
life in the fifty-fourth year of his life and the sev-
enth of his reign." (Antiquities, as cited above)

THE BOOK OF PAUL

13 *MINISTERS OF THE WORD*

(The First Missionary Journey of Paul
13:1-14:28)

ANTIOCH AND CYPRUS MISSIONS 13:1—12

Peter is the dominant character in the first 12
chapters of Acts, thus allowing that section to be ti-
tled "The Book of Peter." There, the Church of

Jerusalem is the center of attention and holds the place of honor, as it always will. Now, the Church of Antioch assumes central importance as a missionary base for the announcing of the Word to the gentiles. If Jerusalem is the doctrinal heart of the Word, Antioch stands as its communications center.

Luke opens with some comments on prophets and teachers. This is a repeat of an earlier idea that the Church had clearly affirmed that the power to be a prophet and teacher was a gift-charism of the Spirit. The 12th chapter of Paul's first letter to Corinth is devoted to the role of such charisms in the Church. This is the enforcement of a theme that the Spirit had given widespread guidance on many facets of the believing community's life. The Spirit's power is present in all phases of Church life.

The liturgical scene in verse two includes the element of fasting as part of opening oneself to the Spirit. The act of fasting as a normal practice of piety recurs constantly throughout the Bible. People instinctively know that fasting is an act of self-purification that both clears the mind and sharpens the sensitivity of the soul to hear the Word of the Lord.

The Antioch community under the leadership of the "Council of Five"—Barnabas, Symeon, Lucius, Manaen and Saul—ponder in prayer their next evangelical move. The Word of the Lord comes to them, "Set apart Barnabas and Saul for me to do the work for which I have called them." Barnabas is mentioned first as he is still the leader of the group. In time the roles will reverse as Saul rises to the first position. To hear the Word is not sufficient. More prayer and fasting is still needed to deepen their spiritual strength. The "laying on of hands" here is not an ordination gesture; it is just a ceremonial sending of the two missionaries.

More must be said here about the hearing of the Word. There is no doubt that the Christians described in the Acts possessed a phenomenal sensitivity to the movement of the Spirit (which also is a way of speaking of the hearing of the Word). To use imagery, this kind of listening appears to be a hearing of the heart. In meditation there is a time for concept making, for mulling over ideas about God and our lives.

This is important and legitimate, but must lead to something deeper, where the interior noise settles down and inner quiet prevails. This is more than a passive waiting. It is a tense attention, waiting, as Thomas Merton once wrote, "to hear the dim drums of Christ the Conqueror." Our busy lives black out the normal practice of inner prayer. We could learn so much from the people of Acts. They also knew what it meant to be busy. The missionary record of Paul would exhaust any modern executive. Always they returned to the dynamism of the Spirit, whom they took time to listen to in prayer, worship and fasting.

Now the first mission journey of Saul begins— setting out from Antioch for Seleucia, a Mediterranean seaport, 16 miles west of Antioch. From there they set sail for Cyprus, where they will find a considerable number of Jews. They arrive at Salamis on the east coast of Cyprus and do some evangelizing in the synagogues. They travel throughout the island, preaching and teaching until they arrive at their main destination, Paphos, on the southwest side of Cyprus.

The main event described here is their encounter with a Jewish magician posing as a prophet. Surprising as it seems, there had been a sub-culture of Jewish magicians, and there are surviving documents to prove it. There is no objection here to the magic, but rather to the pretense of Bar-Jesus to the gift of prophecy. Not really a man of prayer, he is using trickery as a substitute.

Sergius Paulus, the local Roman leader and an intellectual, is anxious to hear what Barnabas and Saul have to say. The magician, now called Elymas (no possible explanation for the name change) seeks to undermine the two apostles. Saul, now officially named Paul in Acts, unleashes a fierce attack on the magician, and inflicts on him, by the power of the Spirit, a temporary blindness. The intensity of Paul's punishing act is reminiscent of the Ananias and Sapphira affair. The story is told quite suddenly for there is no account of the interaction of Paul and Elymas. The assumption must be that he is impenitently standing in the way of the Gospel and Paul is thus moved to strike out at him.

And the proconsul believes.

THE MISSION TO PISIDIAN ANTIOCH 13:13–52

The mission band moves from Cyprus back to the mainland in the southern part of Asia Minor. They debark at Perga in Pamphylia where John Mark leaves them. Paul is displeased with what he feels is a lack of dedication to the mission task. We well know that Paul is a tough-minded and tireless person. He expects a great deal of himself and is equally demanding of others. His comment of John Mark: "But Paul insisted that, as he (John Mark) had deserted them at Pamphylia, refusing to join them on that mission, he was not fit to be taken along now." (Acts 15:38)

They journey on to Pisidian Antioch which is in

southern Galatia. The many Antiochs will seem confusing. The popularity of the name for cities dates back to the time of Alexander the Great. After his death, much of Asia Minor fell to the control of the Seleucid family of whom many princes had been named Antiochus.

The cities usually picked were known for their sizable Jewish settlements. The missionary strategy was to bring the Gospel first to the Jews and then to the gentiles. Normally, they received a mixed reception at the synagogues. They generally made some converts, but as soon as they would turn to the gentiles, those not converted would become quite angry and raise more or less powerful opposition against the missionaries.

From this time on Paul began to emerge as the leader. Historians guess he was at this point about 38 years old. The Acts of Thecla, a second century work, described him as a "sturdy little balding, bowlegged man, with meeting eyebrows and a somewhat hooked nose, full of grace. Sometimes he appeared like a man and sometimes he had the face of an angel." We have no way of really knowing what he looked like, though there may be some merit in the description from Thecla.

His enemies at Corinth said his bodily presence was weak and his speech contemptible. He admitted himself that he was rude in speech, but not in intelligence. His sermons in Acts are not quite the best clue to his preaching, for in the Acts he spoke with the careful outline of a stylized preacher. Turn to his epistles and you get a better idea of how he really preached. His words rushed out like lava from an active crater. He simply burst with the message.

He was not a poet, yet from him came some of

the most exalted words in all of Christian literature. The most notable example was his hymn to
love in I Corinthians 13. There he told of preachers who must do more than speak with the tongues
of angels, for they must burn with love. There is no
question that Paul, one of the greatest religious
figures who ever lived, burned with the love of
Christ to a degree almost unimaginable.

On the Sabbath day, at Pisidian Antioch, they at-
tend the synagogue services. After the readings, the
recitation of the Shema ("Hear O Israel, the Lord is
our God, the Lord alone. Therefore you shall love
the Lord your God with all your heart, and with all
your soul and with all your strength.") (Deut.
6:4), and the 18 blessings, the guests are asked to
preach. Paul stands, in the style of the Greek *rhetor*
(speaker), and not like the rabbi who sat for the
discourse.

His sermon reflects Stephen's use of Old Testament stories of salvation, Peter's account of the
passion and his citing of David to support the fact
of Christ's resurrection. He is well received and
asked back to preach again. Gradually, they make a
number of converts. In time, the whole city acquires an interest in the famous speakers. But once
the gentiles show interest, and Paul and Barnabas
display an equal enthusiasm for converting them,
the old guard who had not accepted the message
are filled with jealousy and move to the attack.

Paul quotes to them from Isaiah 49:6 that the
Word of God would be preached to the gentiles. In
fact, here we have a theme that becomes a sort of
Church strategy. The inability of so many Jewish
Christians to respond to Christ—while a moment
for mourning and regret—has a positive sound, for
it starts the evangelists turning toward the gentiles.

Paul and his sturdy followers were to be the light of nations, a title which Vatican II assigned to the document on the Church.

The gentiles of Antioch receive the Word with joy and glorify the Lord. The old synagogue establishment is not content simply to disagree. They influence the powers-that-be to initiate an harassment of the missionaries. Eventually, the heat is so great that Paul and Barnabas "shook the dust from their feet" and left for Iconium.

14 *JOYFUL MISSIONARIES*

THE ICONIUM MISSION 14:1–7

Iconium—which still exists today as the town of Konia, Turkey—serves as a typical example of the scenario we shall see regularly now. First, the apostles preach at the synagogue. They find a favorable response until gentiles get into the picture, at which point the old guard rebels and institutes serious opposition—"stoning" in this instance. At least in Iconium the opposition must have been growing slowly, for the text says that Paul and the brethren stayed a considerable amount of time.

As always, Paul preaches with "boldness," the courage that Spirit bore. Paul must also have possessed unbelievable physical energy, for he shows no particular signs of exhaustion while he maintains a frightful pace by any standards. "Road lag," the ancient form of jet lag, plus the look of angry faces and the pelting of stones hardly seem to phase him.

In second Corinthians he details his missionary sufferings, not as a complaint, but as a series of tro-

phies that the Spirit had strengthened him to
achieve. (Cf. II Cor. 11:16-29) There he tells of
imprisonments, beatings, five scourgings, a stoning
and three shipwrecks. He withstands danger from
robbers, traitors and his own peoples, in the city, in
the wilderness and at sea. He experiences sleepless
nights, hunger, thirst, exposure to cold and lack of
shelter. Without being irreverent, it is almost a description of a divine superman. Yet we know from
every saint we've ever heard of that the spiritual
power from God makes all this bearable. Christ un-
locks personal resources of strength that no human
prediction could foretell, much less fathom.

THE LYSTRA MISSION 14:8–20

Barnabas and Paul move on another 25 miles to
Lystra. They cure a cripple. The story is told in
very much the same manner as the cure of the cripple at Solomon's Portico. The people of Lystra are
so impressed by the miracle that they think the two
apostles are really the Greek gods Zeus and
Hermes. The text retains the picturesque detail of
the pagan priest bringing garlands to decorate Paul
and Barnabas, as well as oxen to sacrifice to them.

The two apostles decide to put an end to the
unexpected adulation. They tear at their garments
to show their extreme distress at the inappropriate
reaction to their miracle. Paul preaches to them.
Since he is talking only to gentiles, he takes a different approach than when addressing the Jewish
listeners, who know the biblical stories and appreciate the meaning of God in scriptural terms.

Paul launches an attack on idolatry and leads his
audience to the notion of one God, the creator of
all. He permits the gentiles to go their way, even as
he blesses them with rain and harvest and happy

hearts. Paul will give a much more expanded "gentile" sermon when he mounts the rostrum at the Aereopagus in Athens.

The reaction of the people of Lystra remains enthusiastic. They still want to offer sacrifice. This congenial atmosphere soon changes when hostile Jews come from Antioch and Iconium. They stone Paul and leave his presumably dead body outside the walls of the city. But Paul somehow survives the dreadful ordeal of stoning, rises and goes on his way.

DERBE MISSION AND RETURN HOME 14:21–28

They journey to Derbe, 60 miles east of Lystra. The note is brief about their work in Derbe. They make many disciples and endure no further persecution for the time being. The memory of their recent sufferings comes up frequently as they retrace their steps home. They preach perseverance and the necessity of foreseeing and enduring many trials before entering the kingdom of heaven.

This is a message that abides to this day. Soft Christians rely on "cheap grace" to get by, for they do not want to accept the real challenges that faith requires. Bold Christians know that "costly grace," (a term for accepting the high demands of real religion) calls them to solid virtue and decent living and a life of high moral principle. Religion declines both in importance and influence when its leaders and followers forget Paul's example and teachings.

Along the way home they appoint *elders* to oversee the new communities for them. This is another step in the organization of the new Church. We have heard of apostles, deacons, prophets, teachers— and now elders. It shows the sensitivity of the new

Church to both the charismatic as well as the organizational features needed for a future. The new wine of the Spirit needs a new wineskin (organization) to serve and perpetuate the vision and dream that has appeared.

The Church will always need both of these elements. The free-flowing idealists must walk hand in hand with the stabilizing organizers. A river needs banks to guide it. Wine that has no container will be lost. The tension between the idealist and the organizer, the charismatic and the institutionalizer, need not be a negative one. They mutually aid one another's gift from the Spirit who presides over both the gift of himself, as well as a manner in which that gift can be handed on to future generations of the Church.

The exultant apostles finally return home to Antioch and tell the community of their joy in what God has done to bring the Spirit to the gentiles. The door of faith to the gentiles is now definitely open.

15 DECISION IN JERUSALEM

THE APOSTOLIC COUNCIL 15:1–35

Old ideas have a tendency neither to die nor fade away. A certain number of the Jewish converts found it practically impossible to accept the idea that gentiles could become Christians without being circumcised. This group continued to raise the question, cause dissension and humiliate the gentile converts as second-class citizens who most likely would not be saved unless they accepted circumcision.

The growing numbers of gentiles, due to a vigorous missionary effort from the Antioch Church, meant that this controversy was no simple academic debate. A policy for the whole Church had to be settled once and for all. Paul and Barnabas were sent to Jerusalem to meet with the Church there and hammer out an official statement that would be standard procedure in all the churches.

They open a meeting with a report of the first missionary journey and the multitude of new believers, many of them gentiles, whom God had won for them. The issue is joined immediately by the representatives of those Jewish Christians who are convinced that the gentiles must also keep the law of Moses and be circumcised. It must be emphasized here that not all Jewish Christians held this view. As we mentioned earlier, the Spirit was able to open the hearts of many to the new idea that the circumcision mandate was not compulsory for gentiles.

In our case, as we look at this debate, we must not be put off by the prominent detail of the debate which may seem so irrelevant to us. We do not lose sleep wondering whether we should be obeying certain prescriptions of Mosaic Law. The usefulness of the discussion for us is the evidence that profound disagreement about how to live as a Christian occurred at the very origin of our religion.

Barely had the excitement of Pentecost cleared away and the down-to-earth task of building a Church begun, that the question of understanding the new reality faced them. Today we speak of the open and closed mind, of broad and narrow vision, of the personal maturity to perceive the full implications of change. The Acts is a case study of the same problem. People are people after all, with the perennial dilemmas of how to handle new developments and radical change.

At this account of the Apostolic Council, the strong differences of opinion were not hidden behind closed doors, but aired before the whole community. Our own Vatican II saw a similar ventilating of views and a resolution of conflicts that enabled the Church to come to grips with the things to keep in mind when evangelizing the new gentiles in an age of technology, where the idol is not of stone but of steel.

After the Jewish Christians had reasserted their position on making gentiles adhere to the Mosaic Law, Peter responds with a dissenting view. He repeats the substance of the Cornelius event. God has cleansed the hearts of the gentiles with faith, so they could equally receive the Holy Spirit without benefit of Mosaic legal mandates. There is no point in burdening them with cultural forms that appear quite unnecessary.

These were brave and clear words for Peter. Even though he was convinced by the Cornelius happening, he did find himself anguishing over the new approach. Read Galatians 2:11ff. Peter came to Antioch and happily associated and dined with the gentiles. But when some emissaries of the circumcision party came from Jerusalem, Peter withdrew from his gentile associations, both afraid to offend them—and probably wondering if they might be right. Tradition certainly weighed heavy upon him. At the "gut level" he no doubt still favored the ancient way, in spite of his recent conversion to the new.

This is not to characterize him as being unable to act out of principle. It is rather to show, as the

Bible unabashedly does, that the ascent to principle takes time—and painful education. Peter finds himself, red faced, as Paul confronts him on this matter. "The rest of the Jews joined in his dissembling, till even Barnabas was swept away by their pretense. As soon as I observed that they were not being straightforward about the truth of the Gospel, I had this to say to Cephas (Peter) in the presence of all: 'If you who are a Jew are living according to Gentile ways rather than Jewish, by what logic do you force the Gentiles to adopt Jewish ways?' " (Gal. 2:13-14)

At the Apostolic Council we hear a Peter who has worked through the problem. He has received the gift of insight from the Holy Spirit in the house of Cornelius and now has made it his own. He makes his case with convincing simplicity.

And all the assembly kept *silence.* (v.12) This laconic observation is of a piece with an earlier theme that prayer as silent attention was considered a normal part of their deliberations. This gathering was far more than parliamentary procedure or sophisticated debating. It was an hour of discernment which demanded that the noise of men's voices cease from time to time, so that minds might dwell on the Lord and hearts listen to the Spirit.

Then Barnabas and Paul repeat their gentile experience and the work of God among them. Now James, acting as chairman of the assembly, cites the argument of Peter. He calls him Symeon, a variation of Simon, his old name. He argues that Peter's position is well in line with the teaching of the prophets and proceeds to quote from Amos 9:11-12 where a successful mission to the gentiles is predicted.

James then rules that circumcision will not be a requirement for gentiles. However, he does decree that they should give up idolatry, fornication and abstain from blood and strangled animals. These last two details are compromises so that gentiles and Jews (Christians) can eat together in peace. Leviticus 17:10-12 states that Jews should not eat a strangled animal, but one that was butchered and all the blood drained out.

This rule of James was a concession to the sensitivities of the Jewish converts. We must recall that common meals often went together with the house Eucharist, even as today in the case of a home liturgy which is frequently followed by a meal. If the gentiles had not conceded on this custom, then they could never have dined with their Jewish brethren. This rule of James appears to apply only when Jews and gentiles ate together at a mutual feast. Gentiles, in the privacy of their own homes, could follow their own eating practices.

An Apostolic Letter (v. 23-39) officially summarizes the decision of the Council, settling the circumcision problem and noting the concession about meat. Judas and Silas are sent along with Paul and Barnabas to Antioch to deliver the good news. Predictably, it is received with open rejoicing. Comments follow about continual exhortation and strengthening of the people. It is sensed from the very beginning that the life of faith needs constant renewal and invigoration. The style of exhortation is to call, over and over again, the brethren to live up to their vocation, to live in Christ and be ever open to the Spirit.

Paul decides now to embark on another missionary tour. Barnabas wants to bring John Mark along. Paul is against this since John Mark had abandoned their last expedition. Also, Paul is not as enthusiastic about Barnabas either, since he had faltered with Peter on the gentile issue. (Cf. Galatians 2:13-14)

We have noted that Paul was a perfectionist and found it difficult to tolerate lapses in his partners. The Bible seems never embarrassed to portray the human weaknesses of its characters. We fight for it today under the rubric of being honest, open and candid. Scriptural writers apparently took this as a matter of course.

Hence, Paul and Barnabas break up. Barnabas goes his way with John Mark, and Paul invites Silas to be his new partner. They begin with a tour through Syria and Silleia.

16 COME TO EUROPE

(Second Missionary Journey 15:36-18:22)

SECOND VISIT TO DERBE AND LYSTRA 15:1—5

The special event of this trip is the bringing of Timothy aboard as a traveling companion for Paul. Timothy is well spoken of by many of the brethren. As the son of a Greek, he had not been circumcised. But even though it is technically unnecessary now because of the Jerusalem decree, it is felt to be diplomatically helpful, since Timothy will be preaching so often to Jewish communities and hence he can identify better with them. Paul's perfectionism then seems to be related more to the matter of dedicating one's energies totally to the cause and not to rigid disciplinary practices.

PHRYGIA, THE MACEDONIAN VISION 15:6–10

The three missionaries, Paul, Silas and Timothy, attempt to pursue a route into Phrygia, which is in the northern part of Asia Minor. The Spirit blocks their efforts in this regard. Unlike former promptings of the Spirit that have had a positive direction, this is a puzzling negative one, but soon they understand why. They go to Troas, a seaport that looked out on Europe.

That night a Macedonian appears to Paul and appeals to him for help. Paul concludes that this is the will of God to bring Jesus to the Macedonians. Hence, the first Christian mission to Europe begins. They go to Philippi.

THE PHILIPPIAN MISSION 15:11–40

Philippi was named after its founder, Philip II of Macedon. He established it at the site of an ancient village named Crenides, which means tiny spring. Originally a Greek settlement, it was heavily populated by Romans when Paul came there. In 42 B.C. Marc Antony defeated Brutus and Cassius there. By 31 B.C. Octavian made Philippi into a military colony. Basically, it was a soldiers' town, filled with veterans of the many wars that Rome engaged in.

This section sees the text move from the third person to the first person plural, the "we" passages. This means that Luke, the author, was an eyewitness of these events and was thus the fourth member of the missionary group.

Their first convert is a woman named Lydia whose business is selling purple cloth. She insists that Paul and his friends stay at her house while they engage in their ministry.

They encounter next a girl whose profession is

soothsaying (truthsaying). Sort of a super fortune teller, she has been hired by a promotion group and seemingly has brought in a fair income. Like the possessed in the Gospels who had told the truth about Jesus, she finds herself following Paul and his companions and shouting out their true meaning. Paul is annoyed, probably on two accounts. First, that she speaks as from an inner evil spirit. Second, she is very likely a disruptive influence on the authentic line they wish to possess. They do not want their listeners to believe that their work is just a variation of the divination the girl has been so well known for.

After several days of this, Paul resolves to exorcise the girl and he does so successfully. The trouble is that this means the end of the promoters' business. They drag the missionaries before the Roman judge and accuse them of advocating Jewish behavior and customs not in accord with Roman ways. The issue is not very clear. What are the so-called illegal Jewish customs? Probably, they are able to get a conviction on grounds of disturbing the peace.

Paul and Silas are scourged and then put in prison. Now begins a third account of a miraculous escape from jail. Peter had already been freed twice. At midnight the two men sing loud hymns of praise to the Lord. An earthquake shakes the prison and all the doors fly open and the chains unlock. The guard wakes up and thinks his prisoners have escaped.

In Peter's case, Herod had the guards executed for letting their prisoners escape. Here the guard decides to go ahead and commit suicide. Paul stops him in time. No one has escaped. Like the case of Philip and the Ethiopian, we again have a story of "instant conversion." The guard asks what is needed to be saved. He is told and he brings his prisoners home, washes their wounds and has himself and all his household baptized.

The story ends with an unusual detail. The magistrate orders the prisoners released. Paul and Silas must have returned to the jail after baptizing the guard and his family, because he reminds the magistrate that he is a Roman citizen who has been beaten and jailed without benefit of trial. He demands that they come publicly and release him and Silas, as some kind of just redress for the previous humiliation. Since this is in effect a Roman town, their demand is hastily heard and complied with. The question might occur to us, why hadn't Paul insisted on this in the first place before they set upon him and his friend with the rods? There is no way of knowing other than assuming it all happened so suddenly, that even if Paul had protested, he was not listened to the first time.

They return to Lydia's house, make their farewells and embark on the next stage of their evangelical adventure.

17 GOSPEL TO ATHENS

THE THESSALONICAN MISSION 17:1—9

Thessalonica, the capitol of Macedonia, is a port city founded by Cassander, a general under Alexander the Great. Paul, Silvanus and Timothy come to the city to spread the Gospel. They remain about three months and meet with moderate success. The text says "three Sabbaths" but most observers feel it must have been longer, both because of the size of the community that emerged and the importance Paul felt for the group in his two letters to the Church at Thessalonica.

Paul does more than evangelize people. He assumes the responsibility for the administration of the new Churches he founds. Much of this will be done through his famous letters.

It is astonishing, in retrospect, at how well he was able to do this. The communications problem was big enough, given the distances between places, but beyond this was the fact that practically every problem was a new one, meaning that Paul was put in the position of giving "on the spot" solutions that would have historical consequences. His decisions on sex and marriage and on civil authority would influence Christian policy for centuries afterward.

The Thessalonians would eventually raise a knotty problem for him to face. They, like many Christians of the early days, were excited about the second coming of Jesus. This thrilling prospect seemed to be so near that it affected their current lives. A group of them decided that since Christ's triumphant appearance was so close, what was the point of being involved in worldly affairs, of working from day to day, or pursuing a normal life?

Paul, who could speak with flame-like eloquence and idealism, was also a realistic person. He saw his friends using the doctrine of the second coming as an excuse for laziness and a false idea of how to live. He wrote them that the second coming was not so imminent as they would have liked to believe. He concluded with an exhortation to industriousness worthy of a Benjamin Franklin:

"We command you, brothers, in the name of the Lord Jesus Christ to avoid any brother who wanders from the straight path and does not follow the tradition you received from us. You know how you ought to imitate us. We did not live lives of disorder when we were among you, nor depend on anyone for food. Rather, we worked day and night, laboring to the point of exhaustion so as not to impose on any of you." (II Thess. 3:6-8. Read all of chapters two and three of Second Thessalonians.)

During Paul's first visit to Thessalonica, which is the story of our text here in Acts, he met the eventual opposition from a Jewish party. But since they were a real minority group in this city, they were unable to initiate an official persecution. So they used the strategy of innuendo, implying that the Christians were subversives intending to replace the emperor with their own king, Jesus. Because of the precarious hold that Roman emperors had on their thrones owing to revolutions and assassinations, there was usually a sharp reaction to any reports of groups threatening the emperor. Hence, the local authorities were quick to act on the situation. The evangelical group fled to Beroea.

BEROEA 17:10–15

The missionaries are gratefully received by the Beroeans. But the troublemakers from Thessalonica dog their trail and eventually they have to move on.

MEN OF ATHENS 17:16–34

While Athens had passed the peak of its glory when it boasted of philosophers like Aristotle and Plato, of playwrights such as Aeschylus and of the splendid architecture of the Parthenon, it is still a forum for stimulating intellectual discourse. Paul walks through this engaging city, exploring its moods and striving to get the feel of its people. He sees their gods, their idols and notes where they place their ultimate concern. He listens to their poets and philosophers as they expound their view of the meaning of life. He finds secular wisdom at its worst and at its best.

He hears the Epicureans tell him that pleasure is the measure of man so long as it is modified by the life of reason. He converses with hedonists who push the search for pleasure far beyond the bounds of reason advised by the Epicureans. He listens to the Stoics extol the virtues and merits of self-mastery. They urge the crowds to identify with the noblest of ideals, to look proud in the face of defeat and have the good grace never to show pain. Everywhere he finds the repertory theaters recycling the old plays, so that the current generation of Athenians will have something new (though old) to satisfy their abiding curiosity. He strolls through a city of architectural magnificence and sculptured splendor. He is in a cathedral of humanism.

In his conversations with the intellectuals, he keeps bringing up the story of Jesus and the power of his death and resurrection. They put him down by calling him a babbler. But by their own standards, every voice has a right to be heard. They prize freedom of speech. So they bring him to Areopagus, a public forum for exchange of ideas and debate.

Paul's speech has often been termed the sermon on "The Unknown God," a reference to an altar he had found with that inscription. Like any good public speaker he begins where his audience is. He recites the impressions he has received as he has walked through the city and has conversed with the poets and philosophers. He compliments them on being a truly religious people with high ideals. He shows respect and admiration for their intellectual and artistic achievements.

He tries to persuade the listeners to see that his God is the real deity and that future hopes of all men rest on the resurrection of a man whom God has appointed to be the judge of the world.

His sermon was not a startling success. Some mocked him. A few said they would like to hear more about it. A small group, including Dionysius and Damaris, were converted on the spot. This is the last we will hear of the Athenian mission. Paul would write no letters to Athens, probably because the Church never grew large enough to warrant it. Or if they did grow to a considerable size, they apparently raised no problems for him to solve.

He would be far more attentive to the Corinthian Church to the south. His approach at Athens was quite intellectual and rooted in arguments from reason. At Corinth he would find himself repudiating that method, relying more on the declaration of faith in Jesus and the power of the Spirit rooted in that method:

"As for myself, brothers, when I came to you I did not come proclaiming God's testimony with any particular eloquence or 'wisdom.' No, I determined that while I was with you *I would speak of nothing but Jesus Christ and him crucified.* When I came among you it was in weakness and fear, and with much trepidation. My message and my preaching had none of the persuasive force of 'wise' argumentation, but the convincing power of the Spirit. As a consequence, your faith rests not on the wisdom of men but on the power of God." (I Corinthians 2:1-5)

Some see this as a repudiation of the humanistic

method Paul used at Athens. There is no question that Paul, in fact, follows his Corinthian style of evangelization in every other instance. It is hard to say that he would totally reject his Athenian approach, were he to return to that group again and engage them further. Even there we must recall, he moved from reason to faith proclamation of the risen Lord.

18 *TO LIVE LIKE A CORINTHIAN*

THE CORINTHIAN MISSION 18:1–22

These few verses in Acts about Paul's visit to Corinth should be augmented by reading his two letters to the Corinthians, which give a vivid picture of an evolving mission in the Church. Athens, though full of cultural excitement, seemed almost austere when compared to this teeming, sprawling and lively city. Situated in southern Greece, with access to two harbors, it stood in the middle of the shipping lanes of the Mediterranean and was the magnet for the adventurous and the center of mixed populations. It knew the steam of what we would call today "pluralism."

When Paul walked through Corinth he brushed shoulders with government officials, sailors, soldiers, merchants and businessmen from all over the empire. He was impressed with its active sports centers, for there the famed Isthmian games, a sort of local olympics, were held every second spring. Paul must have liked these sports for he often uses game metaphors in his letters.

His eye would also catch the widespread presence of the effects of sexual freedom. Corinth was the sex capital of the world. Popular language would use the expression, "to live like a Corinthian," to mean a person followed the "anything goes" philosophy in sex matters. "Corinthian girl" was a well-known phrase for call girl. The sailors worshipped Aphrodite, from whom they hoped to gain good luck in their sexual adventures. Her temple dominated the city from a 1,700 foot cliff. One account says she had a thousand priestesses serving her—and also servicing the local male population. Paul could amble through an enormous colonade, at the end of which he would see no less than 33 taverns (recently excavated by the American School of Classical Studies).

The text in Acts gives a sparse account, given the actual 18 months that Paul spent in this vibrant city. He lives in the house of Aquila and Priscilla, tentmakers like himself. He loses patience with his Jewish adversaries and hurls at them a traditional Israelite curse, "Your blood be on your own heads!" (v. 6) Yet right after this he converts Crispus, the ruler of a synagogue next to the house of Titus Justus, whose hospitality he is enjoying. Acts notes that God does not want Paul to get discouraged, so he appears to Paul in a dream and fortifies his heart. That aside should be a comfort to all of us, for if the towering courage of Paul needed reassurance, how much more would we.

The vision worked well, for Paul seemed to love Corinth and its possibilities for Christ, so much so that he remained there a year and a half. His epistles tell of the many kinds of problems he faced and solved during his stay. Gentile converts wanted to know if it were still all right to eat the meat sold at Temple butcher shops. The meat had been offered to the gods, thus blessed, and now put on sale. Paul said it was all right in principle, for the gods were simply wood and stone; but that they should not do it in such a way as to scandalize the Jewish converts (thus recalling the decision of the Apostolic Council)—or any of the brethren for that matter.

Widows asked him if they had the right to remarry. He told them that he wished they could remain celibate as he was, but that if their marital needs were so great, "it is better to marry than to burn." Converts asked him about taking their cases to the civil courts. Paul advised them to settle this among themselves by way of gentleman's agreement, thus both excelling in personal charity as well as not airing their dirty linen in the secular form.

When he heard of unruly house liturgies—in which the meals following Eucharists lapsed into carousing and the exclusion of the poorer participants—he angrily attacked the practice, noted that some had died suddenly as a result, and that it gave unforgiveable scandal. It sacrilegiously denied the meaning of Eucharist in the first place.

In a city where love so often meant only sex, Paul exalted their hearts with the greatest poem on divine love ever written, the magnificent canticle to love in I Cor. 13. And it was in Corinth that he developed his teaching on charisms, that the Spirit of God endowed each member of the Church with the special talents used to serve the community, be that of teaching, administration, nursing, preaching and so on. Finally, of special interest for today's Catholic Pentecostals, he devoted a lengthy and thoughtful section to the "gift of tongues." (I Cor. 14)

The text in Acts 18 comments on Paul's continual battle with the synagogue Jews who resent his success and try to block him. They are influential enough to bring him to court before the proconsul Gallio. He seems familiar with the efforts of minority groups to get him to decide in their favor and resolve their disputes. But since he sees no evidence of a real crime, he dismisses the case. There is a puzzling aftermath in which Sosthenes, the ruler of a synagogue, is beaten right before Gallio's eyes, though he pays no attention to this uproar. Was he beaten because he lost the case? Or was it Corinthian Christians who beat him? We will never know for Luke lets the story lie without explanation.

Paul finally leaves Corinth and sails for Syria. At Cenchrae he cuts his hair, for he had taken the Nazarite vow to remain a consecrated person to God (cf. Numbers 6:1-21). He was already obviously consecrated by his baptism and gift from the Spirit, but he retained a loyalty to his Israelite heritage and the custom of the shaved head as a sign of consecration. Christian monks would in later centuries follow a similar practice with their tonsures.

Paul then goes to Ephesus, sails from there back to Caesarea and home to Antioch, finishing the second of his great journeys.

(Third Missionary Journey 18:23-21:14)

APOLLOS 18:23–28

The figure of Apollos is a perennial subject for dilemma and puzzlement. He is portrayed as a cultured person, instructed in the way of the Lord, fervent in spirit and teaching accurately about Jesus. Yet he only knows John's baptism. Furthermore, he preaches with the "boldness" characteristic of Spirit-filled missionaries. How could all this have happened without his knowing Christian baptism and the gift of the Spirit? Perhaps the only reasonable answer is that we are still in a transitional period in the emergence of the new Church. We can suppose that incomplete presentations of Jesus were possible due to the very newness of the Gospel.

What Apollos had known is accurate but not sufficient. Priscilla and Aquila venture to fill in the gaps, and he is enriched by the fullness of the Gospel which he then preaches with even greater fervor. In I Cor. 3 Paul refers to Apollos in his comments on carrying a favorite preacher theme to the point of factions. He is not speaking disfavorably of Apollos, but rather of the persistent tendency of people to be cliquish.

"After all, who is Apollos? And who is Paul? Simply *ministers* through whom you became believers, each of them doing only what the Lord assigned him. I planted the seed and Apollos watered it, but *God made it grow.*" (I Cor. 3:5-6)

19 *ANGRY SILVERSMITHS*

JOHN'S BAPTISM 19:1–7

Paul finds another example of people who had moved as far as John's baptism, but had not yet been enlightened about the Holy Spirit. Paul discloses to them the fullness of Christ. They are baptized and experience a Pentecost of their own.

PAUL PREACHES AT EPHESUS 19:8–20

As always Paul begins in the synagogue until they refuse to listen to him. He continues his preaching at the lecture hall of Tyrannus. Luke describes the miracles wrought through Paul. Once again he reminds that preaching alone is not the full good news. Healing also is considered a very important part of ministry and certainly a good news as well.

Exorcism, too, is a common feature of the healing ministry. The chilling story of the seven sons of Sceva becoming victims of the demons they try to exorcise in the name of Jesus (without faith and commitment to him) is part of the same strand as the "death tales" of Ananias and Sapphira, and the unruly Corinthians at house liturgies—and the blinding of the magician Elymas.

The story of the book burning of the magic arts texts takes up the theme of the confrontation of the Gospel and magic that has already been noted many times. The loss of business for the Ephesian booksellers would naturally lead to an attack on Paul and the Church.

GREAT IS ARTEMIS OF THE EPHESIANS 19:21–40
Ephesus was the center of worship of Artemis (Diana), the goddess of the hunt, of virginity and the moon. An earlier temple in her honor was considered to be one of the seven wonders of the world. Her shrine at the time of Paul's mission to the city was still a splendid place. The text says that local silversmiths had a good business going selling silver replicas of her shrine. Archaeologists have only found terra cotta replicas, so some commentators figure that it was small silver statues of Artemis that were at issue.

In any case, the economic future of the silversmiths would have been bleak if the Christian Gospel had had its way. It is not surprising, therefore, that their anger grows to the point of public riot. They surge to the theater for a public meeting. Luke says that Paul's friends use all their persuasive powers to keep the combative Paul from going down to the theater and entering the rousing debate.

Again we have another puzzling and unanswerable aside in which we are told the Jews put forth a representative named Alexander to stand up and defend his people. Possibly he and his friends are afraid the mob will associate the Jewish community with this hostility to Artemis, and he wants to forestall them. But by now they are at a pitch where the mob spirit wrenches them into chanting, "Long live Artemis (Diana) of Ephesus," for over two hours.

When they had finally exhausted the first phase of their anger, a simple town clerk turns the tide toward reason and peace. He assures them that the government respects the worship of Artemis. There is no record of any desecrations of the Temple. If there is any real legal complaint, they should bring the offenders to the normal magistrates and settle the case in a regular manner.

That seems to satisfy everyone. Mob rule is over and the crowd goes home. Paul, meanwhile, decides in the Spirit to go back to Jerusalem via Macedonia. And now he begins to think of going to Rome.

In conclusion, we can see through the pagan community's violent reaction to the Christians in their midst, that the power of the Spirit was considerable. Pliny the Younger, a Roman governor, wrote in a similar context that the impact of Christianity caused many temples to be deserted, regular services canceled and the sacrificial meat business to decline. (Letter: X. 96 around A.D. 112)

20 FAREWELL, MILETUS

These verses relate a quick outline of Paul's follow-up on the Greek missions. The memorable story from this passage is the death of Eutychus and his consequent resuscitation by Paul. Every student of preaching is reminded that human attention wanes with the length of a talk. Even the eloquence of Paul is not enough to stave off the drowsiness of Eutychus. The result is far worse than mere sleep, as Eutychus falls from the window and dies on the pavement below. Paul miraculously raises the boy to life in the manner of Elijah of the Old Testament, and of Jesus and Peter in the New.

Paul now is hastening home for Pentecost in Jerusalem. He sails the coast of Asia Minor, where he debarks at Miletus and delivers a famed farewell address.

FAREWELL AT MILETUS 20:17–37

This is one of the most beautiful speeches attributed to Paul or to anyone for that matter. It is the kind of talk that any pastor on leaving his flock should consider for the sentiments it contains. Actually, it should be read, not as a pastoral leave-taking, but because of the ideals of pastoral ministry which Paul espouses. We live in a time when the autobiographical in religious literature is achieving a new prominence. The confessional style of an Augustine has returned to make personal our self-declarations about religion and ministry.

Paul's discourse fits very well into this mold. He frankly tells of all the trials and humiliations he has endured to serve the Lord and teach the Gospel. He asserts that he has not been afraid to speak boldly what needed to be heard. He has done this both at public gatherings and in a house-to-house visitation. He knows from the Spirit that ahead of him lies affliction and jail. Bravely, he announces that he is ready to put his life on the line for the sake of Jesus and the Gospel.

Poignantly, he tells them they will see his face no more. He looks at them intently, warning them that after he is gone, people will come and try to ruin what he has established among them. He is under no illusions, for persons will arise to destroy the work of the Spirit. He hopes that his admonition will sharpen their awareness, so they will not be surprised when this happens and will be able to cope with it.

He commends them to God and his grace. He tells them never to forget that he has made no money out of his ministry, for he has worked for what he has received. He has taken care of himself by his own energies. Help the weak and remember, "There is more happiness in giving than receiving."

The closing scene shows them praying and weeping and hugging Paul as they bid him good-bye on his road to the ultimate witness—martyrdom.

21 PAUL'S ARREST

TYRE, PTOLEMAIS, CAESAREA 21:1–14

From Miletus, their boat fairly hugs the Asia Minor coastline moving down to Phoenicia and Syria. Their ship pauses for a week at Tyre to unload some cargo. The missionaries look up some disciples and stay with them. Paul is warned not to go to Jerusalem because the rumors are clear that they mean to kill him. But this does not frighten him. They kneel on the beach and pray with their friends, and then depart for Ptolemais where they remain for one day while communing with the brethren.

They debark for one final stop at Caesarea where they visit with Philip, who now has his four unmarried daughters living with him. They haven't yet received the gift of a husband, but they are endowed with the charism of prophecy. They also meet Agabus again. They had known him from Antioch in the old days when he had become famous for preaching the coming of a worldwide famine, thus spurring the first collection for the Jerusalem Church (Acts 11:28ff).

Agabus reinforces the warnings from the disciples of Tyre. Paul can only hope for death in Jerusalem. Agabus takes Paul's belt and binds his own hands and feet to show Paul what will happen to him in the holy city.

This dramatizing of the message was common among the prophets of the Old Testament. Isaiah shed his clothes and walked nude to illustrate how the Lord would denude Egypt for its war crimes. (Is. 20:2) Ezechiel built a model of the city of Jerusalem and surrounded it with toy siegeworks to show what God would do to the city if they did not repent (Ezechiel 4).

Jeremiah took a waistcloth (an undergarment) and put it in a damp cleft in a rock until it corroded. Then he showed it to the people telling them about the corrosion of soul that their pride was bringing upon them (Jer. 13:1-8). The power and unsettling quality of such prophetic visual aids is lost by the quiet matter-of-fact statements in the scripture. A modern counterpart might be the pouring of animal blood on federal draft records by anti-war people. Whether we agree with them or not, we must admit it attracts attention and drives home a message.

The gesture of Agabus and the pleas of Paul's friends not to put himself in radical danger touch Paul deeply. With a very human touch Paul breaks out, "Why are you crying and breaking my heart in this way?" (v. 13) He insists that he is ready to die for Christ. This has been the noble watchword of all missionaries since Paul's time. This highest form of love has stirred the idealism of generations of young people who have given their lives to the foreign and home missions. It is a courageous dimension of mission endeavor that endures to this day. It prompts our continuing admiration and gratitude. Paul prays with them and they all come to the conclusion of Christ's Gethsemane experience, "The Lord's will be done." (v. 14)

JERUSALEM: ARRIVAL AND ARREST 21:15–40

In Jerusalem Paul is officially greeted by James. The other apostles are no longer mentioned. This may mean that either some or all of them have died by now, or that those who are still alive are off on mission trips. They tell Paul about criticisms that have been leveled against him, especially that he is accused of opposition to the Law of Moses. This scandalizes both Jewish converts to Christianity as well as the non-Jewish community.

The Jewish converts are well aware of Paul's position at the Apostolic Council. He has been faithful and reverent toward the word of God in the

Law of Moses, but he has not agreed that the cultural phenomenon of circumcision is essential to that adherence for gentile converts. They know what he *has* said, but rumors have come to them that he eventually went further and rejected the whole Law.

This is reminiscent of what Kipling wrote centuries later, "If you can bear to hear the words you've spoken twisted by knaves to make a trap for fools. . ." Paul's epistles are filled with statements on the limitations of the Law. Salvation does not come through it, but rather through the grace of Christ in the Spirit. But when he so writes, he is not repudiating the revelation to Moses but showing the fulfillment to which it points. Like Jesus, he does not come to destroy the Law, but to give it the fullest meaning.

In order to dramatically dispel any local misunderstanding, Paul agrees to go through the seven day ritual of the Nazarite vow (v. 27) and even agrees to pay for the sacrificial offerings of four others who are also on a similar kind of "retreat." This is to show that Paul's daring and courage is not so reckless that he is insensitive to the religious feelings of the total Jewish community. If people are going to be hostile to him, they will have to do so for the *right* reasons. Of course, a true enemy is already blinded. They will think him still disloyal to the Law and refuse to see what their eyes tell them. But at least Paul's "act of respect" to the Torah will reassure the open-minded.

Now Paul goes to the Temple with his Ephesian friend, Trophimus, who had been with him on the boat ride completing the third mission journey (cf. Acts 20:4). Paul is seen in the Temple area with this gentile Christian. Paul is, of course, a celebrated person and bound to be recognized. Enemies cry out, accusing him of bringing the gentile into the court of the Jews.

To understand what is going on here, a little description of the Temple and its precincts would be helpful. The locale was mount Zion (or mount Moriah). The top of the mount had been leveled to an area of about 200 yards, the size of two football fields. The Temple building itself, about the size of a large city Church, was situated at one end. Before the Temple building ranged the lengthy esplanade which was basically divided into two courtyards. The one directly in front of the Temple was the court of the Jews. The one behind it was the court of the gentiles.

The Jews worshipped and sacrificed in their own courtyard in front of the Temple. They did not go inside the Temple building. Only the high priest, once a year, entered the Holy of Holies, which was the third innermost room of the Temple. On the Day of Atonement (Yom Kippur) the high priest went into this sacred chamber and offered blood and incense sacrifice. He found there a horned altar, upon which he poured the blood of the sacrificial animal, and then burned sweet incense pleasing to the Lord.

Gentiles, both the pious and the curious, were allowed in an outer court. A prominent stone bulletin board, with inscriptions in Latin and Greek, warned gentiles not to enter the gate leading to the court of the Jews. The punishment for so doing was nothing less than death. That is why the gate leading to the court of the Jews was sometimes called the "thanatos (death) gate". Paul, in writing to the Ephesians told them that Christ had broken down that gate between Jew and gentile, for in the Lord all men could be one.

We don't know whether Paul actually broke the death gate law by bringing Trophimus into the courtyard of the Jews, but at least we know it is used as an excuse to arouse a lynch mob right then and there and so fulfill the warnings Paul had been given on the way to Jerusalem.

The news about the angry mob quickly reaches the fortress Antonia, a Roman guard house, just northwest of the Temple area. A tribune in charge of a cohort, about 600 riot control troops, surges immediately into the Temple area. This had been their normal duty. The history and experience of numerous Temple area riots had prompted the Romans to keep this crack guard on hand.

They reach Paul in time to save him, chain his hands and give him safe conduct to the barracks. The tribune had thought that Paul was the recently escaped Egyptian who had led an attack of 4,000 cutthroats (Sicarians) against the Roman governor in Jerusalem, Felix; the Roman procurator, had met them at the Mount of Olives—just across the valley from mount Zion and the Temple area—and had slaughtered practically all of them. The Egyptian leader had escaped. He and his unfortunate followers had been members of the Zealot party dedicated to eliminating Romans from Palestine. We heard of them earlier in the speech of Gamaliel who spoke of Judas the Galilean and the fate of him and his followers (Acts 5:37)

Paul wants a chance to speak to the crowd. He addresses the tribune in Greek, tells him he is not a renegade Egyptian but rather a Jew from Tarsus. He persuades the startled tribune to permit him to talk to the mob. Paul raises his hand in a rhetorical gesture and hushes the people.

22 "I WILL SPEAK OF VISIONS"

TEMPLE SPEECH 22:1–30

Paul's ability to stand up and give a calm conciliatory speech after having been beaten, let alone facing the waves of hate stares they shot at him, is a tribute again to the Spirit's gift of boldness and courage to the "vessel of election." In the Spirit Paul is able to turn his enemies around to listen one more time to an announcement of the Gospel.

Luke says he speaks to them in Hebrew. Most likely this was a dialect of Hebrew, namely, Aramaic. Paul respects their language and wins their attention by using it. He then launches into autobiographical details about his training under Gamaliel here in Jerusalem. He admits he had been a ruthless agent of the religious establishment against the Christians.

He tells the story of his conversion (Luke's second account) adding some new details, such as that it happened at noon. This is to dispel any misunderstanding that it had been a night vision. He says his companions see a light but hear no one. In Acts 9:7 they hear a voice but see nothing. We have no way of reconciling these contradictory statements.

Again in a conciliating mood, Paul portrays Ananias almost as a Jewish prophet, attributing the conversion of Paul to the God of our Fathers. Paul says he went into ecstasy. Commentators tend not to identify this ecstasy with the one Paul tells of in second Corinthians. Still we do get a clue of what his ecstasy might be like from his words there:

"I must go on boasting, however, unless it may be,

and speak of visions and revelations of the Lord. I
know a man in Christ who, fourteen years ago,
whether he was in or outside his body I cannot say,
only God can say—a man who was snatched up to
the third heaven. I know that this man—whether
in or outside his body I do not know, God knows—
was snatched up to Paradise to hear words which
cannot be uttered, words which no man may
speak." (2 Cor. 12:1-4)

Paul then confesses his cooperation in the martyrdom of Stephen. Next Paul announces his call
from God to be an apostle to the gentiles. That
breaks the spell. Standing in the shadow of the
death gate, Paul reminds them of why they had,
moments ago, tried to lynch him. They immediately recover their murderous intent. Yelling for
blood, throwing fistfuls of dust in the air and
snapping their flowing garments, they demand his
execution.

The tribune, Claudius Lysias (Acts 23:26), takes
Paul away from the uproar and orders the customary scourging-torture for getting information out of
prisoners. In Acts 16 we saw that Paul was beaten
and jailed before he protested his right as a Roman
citizen to a trial and sentencing before any brutal-
ity could be inflicted. This time he makes his protest prior to the scourging.

Claudius is amazed that Paul had gained his citizenship by birth, for he had to pay a large sum for
his citizen's privilege. We are not told how Paul
proves his citizenship, given the lack of papers and
the distance from his home. Apparently his word is
enough.

The tribune unbinds Paul, puts him under pro-
tective arrest and plans an unofficial meeting with
the Sanhedrin. It is unofficial because his low rank

does not give him the authority to summon the Sanhedrin. They seemingly concur because they want every chance to discredit Paul.

23 CLOAK-AND-DAGGER ESCAPE

PAUL MEETS THE SANHEDRIN 23:1—10

Paul's meeting with the Sanhedrin is one of the strangest recorded in Acts. First, he barely has affirmed that, after all, he is living by his conscience, and Ananias tells those near Paul to slap him in the mouth. Why? No one knows. Paul's conscience statement is fairly bland and hardly provocative. The "out of order" striking of Paul brings an equally violent response.

Paul curses the high priest as a hypocrite, a white-washed wall, echoing Christ's similar condemnations in Matthew 23:27. The others are shocked and ask Paul how he could speak so to a high priest. Paul's reply must be seen as sarcastic or ironical since he obviously knows the identity of Ananias, yet with injured innocence he claims he doesn't realize it. Paul adds salt to the ironical wound by quoting the Torah text that forbids reviling high priests.

More oddly yet, Paul decides to divide his listeners on the issue of resurrection. He links the Christian doctrine of resurrection with the Pharisee's belief in the rising from the dead. The Sadducees in the room deny resurrections, spirits and angels. Thus Paul diverts their attention from him by throwing them into a quarrel about their own religious divisions. What is Paul trying to do? Is he tired of defending himself? Is he really trying to get the Pharisees on his side?

We will never know. One thing is certain: the explosive issue he raises made the group sufficiently irrational that they are about to turn on him anyway. So Claudius has Paul taken back to the barracks. As so often in the Acts, these tumultuous events are then backed away from and the reflection on the life of the Spirit reintroduced. The Lord comes and stands by Paul and gives him courage. He need not worry for he shall be protected so that he can testify to Christ in Rome.

AMBUSH AND SAFE CONDUCT TO CAESAREA 23:11–35

The story at this point takes a cloak-and-dagger turn. The frustrations of the Sanhedrin are relayed to the enemies of Paul in the city. Forty activists come together and conspire to assassinate him, dramatically vowing neither to eat nor drink until he is destroyed. The text then introduces an unusual family note. We hear that Paul has a nephew living in Jerusalem.

There has been speculation as to how Paul's devout Pharasaic family had reacted to Paul's conversion. He had gone to see them after the Damascus experience, but nothing is said about how they had received him. At least, it can be said that his nephew is on his side. Somehow he hears the story of the murder plot and conveys it to Claudius. The tribune decides that Paul must be mysteriously spirited out of the city to safety in Caesarea.

Claudius uses the ruse of a military convoy. He has Paul dressed as a cavalry soldier with cloak, helmet and horse. Thus attired, Paul rides from Jerusalem, surrounded by 200 infantry men with swords and shields, 200 spearmen and seventy horsemen.

Hence, the conspirators prowling the streets and suburbs of Jerusalem see, at nine o'clock at night, half the cohort from the Antonia heading for the Caesarean road. They do not suspect this is a prisoner's escort. They probably imagine it is an emergency foray against some new uprising. Also, with half the cohort gone, they rejoice at the thought they will have an easier time getting through to their target.

But Paul the Roman citizen, incongruously dressed in an imperial uniform, smilingly rides to Caesarea. In Ephesians 5 he will describe the power of Christ in terms of shields and breastplates that withstand the fiery darts of the enemy. He gets firsthand experience of this on that night when he sees the moonlight playing on the Roman armor and helmets, of which he wears one himself. But for him, the helmet is an image of divine, not just human, salvation.

Claudius sends a letter to Felix the governor of Caesarea, explaining why Paul is being transferred to new custody. He mentions both the plot against Paul and the rights of Paul as a Roman citizen. Paul goes through the formalities and is told by Felix that they will have an official meeting when his accusers inevitably arrive.

24 *DEFENSE BEFORE FELIX*

PAUL AND FELIX 24:1–27

The accusers in fact arrive five days later. It is a high-quality delegation headed by the high priest Ananias and a shrewd lawyer, Tertullus. The lawyer begins by flattering Felix, complimenting him for his victory over the Zealots at the Mount of Olives massacre, and for his program of social reforms on behalf of the Jews.

In his case against Paul, Tertullus cites the apostle as a world revolutionary, traveling everywhere to stir up Jews against Rome. He characterizes Paul as the leader of the sect of Nazarenes. By classifying Paul as a sect chief, he puts Paul in the position of being part of a heretical group within Judaism, rather than the leader of Christians, a totally new religion. Tertullus concludes his argument by alleging that Paul profaned the Temple by breaking the death gate rule in bringing Trophimus into the court of the Jews. Tertullus uses a smooth, underplayed, soft-sell approach.

Paul's defense is equally urbane. He is not above beginning with some flattery himself. He reminds Felix that he knows the governor has had the longest tenure in this job since Pilate. This is a tribute to his competence as an administrator, surviving so well where so many others had failed. Paul is very much at ease: "I am thus encouraged to make my defense before you." (v. 10)

Paul starts with the Temple accusation. He notes that, first of all, he is only there 12 days, hardly enough time to get a sedition going. Secondly, he had not gone to Jerusalem for traitorous purposes. He had gone as a pious pilgrim, spending seven days in retreat according to the purification rites of the Nazarites. His only other purpose for being in Jerusalem had been to bring alms which he had collected for the community there.

Secondly, Paul builds on the accusation that he is a member of a Jewish sect. He accepts the characterization and stresses those aspects of Christianity that are in continuity with Judaism. The same God is worshipped. The same belief in resurrection from the dead is professed. He skillfully ties in the Pharisee religious belief about resurrection with its continuance among Christians. Hence, by locating Christianity within the context of Judiasm he accomplishes two things. He gives his Jewish listeners another chance to see their possible fulfillment in Jesus. He retains for Christianity the legal protection that Rome affords to Judaism.

Later, as Rome and Christianity itself become finally conscious of their radical independence from Judaism, this legal protection will vanish, and the famed Roman persecutions aimed at exterminating Christians will begin. We have alluded to this evolution earlier, showing that once the Temple is destroyed then Christians will have made their final break with Judaism. They will have moved out of the shadow of the Temple into the light of their own independence. Paul's dwelling on identification with Judaism is probably the reason why he says nothing here about his mission to the gentiles.

Felix defers any judgment on the case until he hears from the tribune, Lysias, directly. He puts Paul under house arrest. Paul is allowed regular visitors, and all his normal needs can be met. This procedure is to last for two years. Felix and his Jewish wife, Drusilla, come to visit Paul off and on. He wants to know about faith in Jesus. Felix is comfortable as long as Paul stays on the topics of Jesus' life and death and resurrection, but when he turns to Christ's moral teaching about justice, self control and future judgment, Felix grows nervous and stops meeting with Paul.

The problem was that Felix was married to a divorced woman. She had been married to Azizus, the king of Emesa in Syria. Felix seduced her away from her husband and brought her into this adulterous union. Small wonder he squirmed as Paul talked of self-control and acting with integrity. The text says that Felix anticipated Paul would try to bribe his way out of jail. Paul's words about bringing alms to Jerusalem caused Felix to think the apostle probably had access to funds that could buy his release.

Two years passed. According to Roman law, Paul should have been automatically released at this point since no judgment was rendered. Instead Felix ignored the law. His own tenure was up. He passed the case onto Festus, the new governor.

25 APPEAL TO CAESAR

PAUL AND FESTUS 25:1—12

Now the legal maneuverings come to a stop. Festus is a decisive man who wants this case cleared up. A Jewish delegation had asked for a hearing in Jerusalem. Their plan is to ambush him on return and settle the matter once and for all. Festus investigates the situation. He is willing to have a Jerusalem trial, but he knows that he will have to settle the case himself in the last analysis.

Festus asks Paul about his submitting to a Jerusalem hearing. Paul refuses. He knows that he has already been treated unjustly by Felix. He realizes the seriousness of putting himself at the mercy of a court in Rome, which could very well sentence him to death. But Paul fearlessly demands an imperial trial. "I appeal to the emperor." (v. 11)

Paul uses the legal affirmation to set in motion a spiritual mission, for he wants to bring Christ right to the imperial city itself. Thus, the Gospel will be brought finally to the "ends of the earth." What had begun in Jérusalem, had expanded to Antioch and had flooded in Cyprus, Macedonia, Athens, Corinth and Ephesus would now stream at last to the center of the empire. Paul will speak of Christ, his Cross and resurrection in the streets and palaces of Rome itself.

AGRIPPA VISITS FESTUS 25:13–27

Paul must wait until Festus writes up a proper report for the Roman authorities. During the delay a distinguished guest arrives. It is King Agrippa II and his sister, Bernice. This king is the great grandson of Herod the Great. He no longer has much territory to rule. He controls a section of Syria, some land on the north side of the lake of Tiberias and a few small territories outside of Palestine. Festus tells his guests about Paul. They show a special interest in meeting him. Festus obliges readily, hoping the meeting will help clarify the report he must write.

26 *AGRIPPA*

PAUL AND AGRIPPA 26:1–32

The setting is described in colorful royal terms. Like a Shakespearean play in which king and retinue enter, Agrippa and Bernice come to hear what Paul has to say. His speech is in three parts, including all the themes with which we are now familiar.

The first part takes up the direction Paul has been using in his debate with the Sanhedrin, doing everything he can to show the religious connection between the tradition of the Torah as mediated by the Pharisees—especially on the question of resurrection and the worship of the same God of the patriarchs. Paul feels comfortable in taking for granted all the Torah allusions, since he knows Agrippa understands even though he is not a believing Jew.

Then Paul reviews his persecutions of the Christians and follows this with the story of his conversion. This is the third account in Acts. Verse 14 contains the famous statement about Christ telling Paul not to kick against the goad for that is useless. A goad was a sharp prong used to keep cattle in line. Christ is determined that Paul should be his apostle and keeps goading him until he gives in. The major departure from the other conversion stories is that Paul does not mention the role of Ananias. In this account the Lord himself tells Paul that he should go and evangelize the gentiles.

The last section of Paul's talk tells about his preaching the Gospel of repentance and the cause of his arrest in the Temple. He concludes by proclaiming the necessity of Christ's passion and resurrection as a prelude to spreading the light to all nations. This echoes Luke's story of the road to Emmaus where Jesus tells the grieving apostles that it is necessary that Christ suffer and enter into his glory.

Festus blurted out that Paul sounded like a madman. Festus was no expert on these mideast religions. Probably, the talk about resurrection caused him to criticize Paul, whom he otherwise considered a learned man. Paul appealed to Agrippa, knowing that the king was well aware of the religious theory of Judaism. None of this would be too surprising to him. He would certainly know the story of the suffering servant in Isaiah 53 and would be intrigued by Paul's implicit application of this to Jesus.

Agrippa says that he doesn't want to hear Paul any longer for he might succumb and become a Christian. It is not clear whether this is said jokingly or seriously. What is more puzzling though is his aside to Festus upon leaving the scene. They all agree Paul has done nothing to deserve death. And Agrippa enigmatically adds that it is too bad Paul appealed to Caesar because he could easily be freed right now.

So the question arises, what legal nicety stops them from releasing him anyhow? The report isn't written yet. Rome knows nothing about Paul. Why doesn't Festus follow his conscience? Is it that once Paul officially and ritually demands an imperial trial, he must get one willy-nilly?

Whatever the reason the die is cast. Paul will sail for Rome in any event. His heart is eager to tell the Romans about Christ. His heart's desire will be fulfilled.

27 *SHIPWRECK*

PAUL SAILS FOR ROME 27:1–44

Considering that biblical figures were not a seafaring people, this chapter on the voyage of Paul is remarkably detailed. Luke is with him, as we can tell from the "we" passages. He writes a vivid account of the whole trip. Festus assigns Paul to sail with a group of prisoners destined for Rome. Julius of the Augustan Cohort takes charge of them. As is soon evident, this is the wrong time to sail. They leave in mid-September as can be inferred from Paul's reference to the Fast (v. 9), a preparation for the Day of Atonement, which normally is celebrated anywhere from mid-September to early October.

Usually, no voyages were made from November 11 to March 10 because the weather was too rough. When they sailed, they followed the custom of hugging the shoreline as closely as possible. Even then, sailing was a dangerous and treacherous business. Luke's detailed story must have resulted from his careful questioning of what the sailors were doing along the way.

Their first stop is at Sidon in Phoenicia. Paul debarks and visits his friends for the last time. Luke notes that Julius, the man in charge of the prisoners, was a humane and tolerant guard. Then they sail past Cyprus, westward to Italy. They dock at Myra on the south coast of Asia Minor. They change ships and board an Alexandrian boat that is heading for Italy. They pass by the island of Rhodes and come to the island of Crete.

They pause at Fair Havens, in the south of Crete. Paul wants them to stay there for the winter. He knows enough about voyaging to foresee that everything might be lost if they proceed. The centurion consults the ship captain and owner, who says the harbor at Fair Havens is not good for wintering. Better to go to the north side of the island and winter there.

They should have listened to Paul. Instead the centurion approves moving on. A south wind comes that would have moved them north as they wished. But soon, as they should have expected, a storm arises with a violent northeastern wind. It drives them away from land and far off their intended course. They do whatever they can to secure the ship. They lower the anchor to serve as a kind of brake. They throw a good deal of the wheat cargo overboard. The storm hides the sun and stars for days. With no way to navigate, they are hopelessly lost and begin to lose hope.

Then Paul gives them a speech one day. His opening words are worthy of a scolding schoolmarm. "Men, you should have taken my advice." (v. 21) If their reactions are at all natural, they are probably ready to throw Paul overboard for his blunt reproval. At any rate, he goes on with an encouraging statement that an angel had appeared to him and had told him that the ship would be lost, but that all on board would be saved. Again, as in every other story in Acts, the divine dimension is present. As Christ's saving presence had been in the midst of a storm on the lake of Galilee, so the Lord's saving hand would help this Alexandrian crew and its passengers to arrive safely at shore.

Two weeks of this pass until the sailors feel they are nearing land. They take soundings and agree land is nearby. They wish it were morning, so they could avoid the rocks. The story says they lowered a boat into the sea with the intention of escaping now and abandoning the passengers. This is puzzling, for they would not be able to avoid the rocks in the middle of the night any more with a small boat than with a big one. They must have panicked. Paul tells the centurion about their plan. His soldiers cut the ropes and the little boat floats away.

At daybreak Paul speaks to them about how hungry everyone is. During the storm it had been impossible to eat. Now with the comparative calm, they should eat and gain some strength. He takes bread and says grace and eats. The others follow his example. Some note that the text has him taking the bread and praying as though for a Eucharist. But given the situation, this could hardly be so.

The remaining wheat cargo is thrown into the sea. They prepare to beach the boat. They throw away the anchors, loosen the rudders and raise the sail. Unfortunately, they hit a shoal. The stern breaks and the surf crashes against the remainder of the boat. The terrified soldiers decide to kill the prisoners. We have already noted this grim responsibility of prison guards. The humane Julius stops them for he wishes to save Paul. He orders those who can swim to go first. The others are told to grab a plank and make for shore. In this way all are saved, just as Paul foresaw.

28 *FROM MALTA TO ROME*

HOSPITALITY AT MALTA 28:1–10

They discover they have landed at Malta. They are cordially received and treated well. While Paul is fixing a fire, a serpent jumps on his hand and stays there. Paul simply shakes it off into the fire. The observers feel sorry for him, for they anticipate he will die from snakebite. They figure that since he is a prisoner destined to die and because the sea had not gotten him, the snake would. When nothing happens to him, they revise their position and conclude he is a god. This parallels the same reaction to Paul and Barnabas at Lystra, only this time they do not embarrass Paul by wreathing him with garlands and preparing to offer a bull in sacrifice to him. (Cf. Acts 14:11)

Paul accepts an invitation to the house of Publius, the island chief. Paul heals the father of Publius and then also heals others on the island who come to him for care. The ministry of healing is good news that supplements the Gospel preaching. The Malta interlude ends with Paul receiving presents and warm farewells.

THE OLD SAINT COMES TO ROME 28:11–31

They board another Alexandrian ship that bears carvings of the twin brothers, Castor and Pollux, on the prow. These deities have been loved by sailors as protectors from storms. They stop at Syracuse on the coast of Sicily, at Rhegium—a town on the tip of Italy's boot—and finally at Puteoli on the Gulf of Naples. This is a traditional port of entry to Italy from the islands. Paul is met by the local Christian community and stays with them for a week.

Then he makes the overland journey to Rome. The Roman Christian community hears of his coming. They are so delighted at his coming that they go 40 miles outside of Rome to the Appian Forum and the Three Taverns to give him a joyous welcome. They first see Paul as a prisoner in chains, but their happy surging about him makes his arrival in Rome something akin to a triumph.

Paul is allowed to rent his own lodgings. A soldier is assigned to guard him. Three days later, Paul invites Jewish leaders to his house and explains how he came to be here, why he is under house arrest and why he is awaiting trial. They reply they had heard none of this before and are anxious to hear more about his "sect." They seem unaware of Christianity, yet a Christian group obviously exists in Rome. They promise to come back and hear more.

Paul announces the Gospel to them on their return. As in every other missionary experience he has had, he finds some accept Jesus with open hearts and others do not. Once again he faces members of his ancestral religion who will not accept the new message. He tells them that the Holy Spirit has been quite correct in speaking through the prophets who had foreseen that the Gospel would sometimes meet a hard heart and a deaf ear from the very ones who should have accepted it first. Paul concludes by informing them of the mission to the gentiles.

Paul lives at his place for two years at his own expense. He spends all his time joyously preaching the kingdom of God and teaching about Jesus. He does so openly and without hindrance.

It was there that he wrote his warm letters to the Philippians and Colossians and to Philemon. He was now the old veteran of the Christian mission. Those last three letters tell us of the abiding affection he had for the members of the Church. He wrote the Philippians of how he held them deeply in his heart, praying for them night and day. Touchingly he assured the Colossians that he was not too old to write his own letters. "This greeting is from Paul in my own hand! Remember my chains. Grace be with you." (4:18) To Philemon he confided the care of Onesimus, a former slave. He also said that Philemon should be sure to save the guest room for him when he visits again, which of course, will never happen.

Paul had the pleasure and comfort of spending his last days surrounded by many friends from his numerous missionary encounters. There is no record of his trial. Most likely he and Peter were both martyred during the persecution of Nero after the great fire of Rome in July of 64.

Paul does not speak much of the historical life of Jesus, but he is evidently in union with the risen Christ. To be "in Christ Jesus" is a constant motto of Paul. In the Acts he is always seen as vibrant with the power of the Spirit. This is all the more remarkable when we see what a stubborn human psychology he had. No question but that he had plenty of self will and all the possible pitfalls of the exhaustive activist. It is all the more astonishing then, that he could place his bony and resistant psychology at the service of the Spirit. Once that marvelous mix of strong-willed radical and grateful, open-hearted Spirit took place, the stuff of the world's greatest missionary took place.

His message along with Peter's—and therefore of the Acts—is that the Spirit of Jesus provides the world with the most real of all revolutions, better than any provided by intellectuals, or militarists or scientists. We shall be saved by Jesus in the power of the Spirit. No chains need bind the world, for there is a freedom in Christ. "It was for liberty that Christ freed us . . . A man will reap only what he sows . . . if his seedground is the Spirit, he will reap eternal life." (Galatians 5:1; 6:8)

It is a grace to know the story of the Acts of Peter and Paul and all the missionaries who had aided Christ's message to come alive because they had been responsive to the Spirit. We can only hope that our present gratitude will create open hearts in our own time to feel again the incredible call that moved the first messengers of the Gospel to touch us and prompt us to take to the road under the power of the Spirit. We ask this favor from the Lord. Amen.

CONCLUSION

The Acts of Peter and Paul and all the fascinating cast of characters who parade through the story of the first Christians call us to review our own relation to the Holy Spirit. It is clear that the mighty deeds of these mighty people proceed from the inner gift of power that has come to them from God's Spirit. We would do well to rediscover their secret. The dynamism of the Spirit rests in the heart of our Church and is available to every human heart.

We live in a period of history when the powers of human invention are astonishing. Technology presents us with a never-ending feast. The meal is, in fact, so rich that we suffer from scientific indigestion, or "future shock" as Alvin Toffler so well named it. Besides this we also suffer from a host of other social evils: crime in the streets, alcoholism in the suburban home, drug addiction in the middle class schools, hunger and poverty in the world's richest nation, a divorce rate that threatens soon to dissolve 50% of all marriages, and abortion on demand.

Religion and religious value must speak strongly to these social and moral catastrophes. But sometimes religion, too, has preached the modern myth that man is really superman, meaning that the human is the sole creator of all that is. The way this comes out among some people in religion is this: God has granted the human the power of developing creation. Man is the inheritor of the earth and is expected to till and manage it. God leaves us to the job, having given us the tools of intelligence and imagination and the raw material of planet earth.

But this is just a half-truth. It is a kind of secularism with a religious beginning. God starts things. We finish them without any further reference to him other than a grateful "thank you" for a good start. Why did this kind of thinking creep into religion? For one thing, this is the spirit of the times. Man is the center and God is on the perimeter.

Secondly, religion has been accused of not respecting the human enough. Religion has been told that it frustrated "self-startership" in people. It must be admitted that the critics do have a point. Religion does sometimes keep people in an escapist world where human energy, intelligence and imagination lay stagnant and underdeveloped.

The criticism is right. The solution is wrong. Human creativity certainly must develop to its most shining potential. But God does not leave us alone in this task. He has sent his Son Jesus to us to show us that humanity reaches its most glorious development when it is in profound unity with the divine at all times. Jesus sends the Spirit to us to help us achieve the same kind of goal.

How pertinent is the ancient prayer of the Church: "Come Holy Spirit and fill the hearts of your faithful. And *you* shall renew the face of the earth." How relevant, therefore, is a review of the Acts, which is a case study of people who were at once magnificently human and gloriously seized by the divine.

Do you want to see human creativity in action? Look at Paul who never flinches at facing and solving a host of problems, everyone of which is practically brand new. Do you want an example of human boldness, courage and ultimate witness? Read the story of Stephen who looks straight into the eye of the storm of opposition and speaks his piece. And he still has the presence of mind to forgive those who pound his body to death.

Are you looking for leadership qualities? Review the case history of Peter who leads the tiny community from the Upper Room and out into a vigorous Palestinian ministry. Peter has the good grace to yield on the divisive issue of circumcision, and goes to Rome to die on a cross.

Is it social concern that captures your imagination? Underline the stories of healings, the establishment of deacons (a social service group), exorcisms, resurrections and the exposés of magicians who are cheating the poor.

Is it human warmth, affection and sentiment that tugs at your questing heart? Blue pencil in your scriptures the enormously affectionate farewell speech of Paul at Miletus (Ch. 20:17-28)

Even if you're looking for human orneriness, the Acts offer plenty of data. Paul is particularly adept at this, especially in his breakup with Barnabas and his petulant scolding of the sailors on the fateful trip to Malta.

Yes, there is plenty of humanity in the Acts, both the peaks and depths thereof. But it is equally clear that there is plenty of Holy Spirit, too. This is no story of an absentee God who leaves us to do the work that he has started. We are not computers left by God to write our own printouts. In real religion the divine and the human are profoundly intertwined. As long as this is so, the human will grow to proper maturity and the divine will be disclosed in both the small and great events of life.

Modern life wants to keep God out of the picture for fear he will upset probability curves, balances of power, the "integrity" of human learning. In Acts we discover a world where the presence of God is as natural as air, water and sun—and there is no fear he will interfere with the progress of human maturing. In fact the opposite is the case. Should he abandon the human, it would face destruction (one of the special meanings of the Malta naval trip).

There have been cultures and ages in the Church where the Spirit of the Acts pervaded the consciousness of people. And they have prospered quite well indeed. Arts flourished, agriculture developed, cottage industries grew and the groundwork for modern science was established. The Acts is a challenge to us to create a culture where the Spirit of God is a ready, available and powerful presence of everyone.

We cannot create this alone. Acts began in the Upper Room with nine days of intense prayer for his coming. Today we need hundreds, perhaps thousands, of Upper Room experiences. Our world requires the coalescence of a huge prayer effort to beg mightily the onrush of the Spirit of Jesus. We will need more than nine days. We will need "prayer without ceasing." Recall the old, but relevant, words of Tennyson, "More things are wrought by prayer than this world knows of."

In Acts they do not stop praying after the Upper Room event. They pray in homes, in prisons, on shipboard, by seashores, in open markets, by Temple gates, at the Forum of Appius—and even in the shadow of "Three Taverns." (Acts 28:15-16) When our prayer becomes as regular as our breathing then we begin to create the "atmosphere" for the arrival of the Spirit. Jesus has told us that if we pray for the Spirit, he will come. The Acts is exhibit "A" that such prayer is always answered.

Reemphasizing the need for prayer and the Spirit and the divine dimension of life does not ask us to practice denial of the modern world and its technological wonders. To turn to God is not to devalue the human. The Indian mystic Sri Auribindo, mentor of Gandhi, once wrote, "In the old days the monks fled the world to reach God. Today the new monks go to God that the world might leap with divine vitality and achieve human maturity."

Our secular doomsdayers put it better than anyone. They tell us that human creation has now become so skilled that it can be self destructive. We have bombs and poisons and bacteria that can hurl us back to the stone age—if not wipe us out completely. In charge of these fateful toys we have people who lack any sense of God and appear to have lost all hold on the value of human life and moral values. No religious critic could say it better.

The critique of religion has been that it produces people who are not human enough. While religion should humbly admit this when it is true, it might also candidly point out that the non-religious culture has been fairly skillful at dehumanizing as well.

Religion should not forget the lesson about the need to build the human. But it must also remember that this is best done, as our sturdy forefathers in the Acts have taught us, by willfully and enthusiastically staying in contact with the Holy Spirit. Certainly, we must use the insights of the behavorial sciences and the analyses of the social critics. But this must be done within the Christian value system.

We must be souls on fire. We will be warm so long as we stay near the fire. The existentialist philosophers have told us we are alienated, we are cold souls, citizens of a lonely crowd. Why should we be so lonely when Jesus has given us the greatest advocate (the word also means laywer) and friend in the Spirit. The old revival hymn states, "What a friend we have in Jesus." The hymn of Acts extends this sentiment: "What a friend we have in the Spirit!"

DISCOURSES

Peter's Message on Pentecost
Acts 2:14-36

Then Peter stood up with the other eleven apostles, and in a loud voice began to speak to the crowd, "Fellow Jews, and all of you who live in Jerusalem, listen to me and let me tell you what this means. These men are not drunk, as you suppose; it is only nine o'clock in the morning. Rather, this is what the prophet Joel spoke about,

'This is what I will do in the last days, God
     says:
  I will pour out my Spirit upon all men.
Your sons and your daughters will prophesy;
     your young men will see visions,
     and your old men will dream dreams.
Yes, even on my slaves, both men and women,
     I will pour out my Spirit in those days,
     and they will prophesy.

I will perform miracles in the sky above,
and marvels on the earth below.
There will be blood, fire, and thick smoke;
the sun will become dark,
and the moon red as blood,
before the great and glorious Day of the
Lord arrives.
And then, whoever calls on the name of the
Lord will be saved.'

"Listen to these words, men of Israel! Jesus of
Nazareth was a man whose divine mission was
clearly shown to you by the miracles, wonders, and
signs which God did through him; you yourselves
know this, for it took place here among you. God,
in his own will and knowledge, had already decided
that Jesus would be handed over to you; and you
killed him, by letting sinful men nail him to the
cross. But God raised him from the dead; he set
him free from the pains of death, because it
was impossible that death should hold him prisoner.
For David said about him,
'I saw the Lord before me at all times;
he is by my right side, so that I will not be
troubled.
Because of this my heart is glad
and my words are full of joy;
and I, mortal though I am,
will rest assured in hope,
because you will not abandon my soul in the
world of the dead;
you will not allow your devoted servant to
suffer decay.
You have shown me the paths that lead to life,
and by your presence you will fill me with
joy.'

"Brothers: I must speak to you quite plainly about our patriarch David. He died and was buried, and his grave is here with us to this very day. He was a prophet, and he knew God's promise to him: God made a vow that he would make one of David's descendants a king, just as David was. David saw what God was going to do, and so he spoke about the resurrection of the Messiah when he said,

'He was not abandoned in the world of the dead;

his flesh did not decay.'

God has raised this very Jesus from the dead, and we are all witnesses to this fact. He has been raised to the right side of God and received from him the Holy Spirit, as his Father had promised; and what you now see and hear is his gift that he has poured out on us. For David himself did not go up into heaven; rather he said,

'The Lord said to my Lord:

Sit here at my right side,

until I put your enemies as a footstool under your feet.'

"All the people of Israel, then, are to know for sure that it is this Jesus, whom you nailed to the cross, that God has made Lord and Messiah!"

Stephen's Message Before the Council
Acts 7:2-53

Stephen answered, "Brothers and fathers! Listen to me! The God of glory appeared to our ancestor Abraham while he was living in Mesopotamia, before he had gone to live in Haran, and said to him, 'Leave your family and country and go to the land that I will show you.' And so he left the land of

Chaldea and went to live in Haran. After Abraham's father died, God made him move to this country, where you now live. God did not then give Abraham any part of it as his own, not even a square foot of ground; but God promised that he would give it to him, and that it would belong to him and his descendants after him. At the time God made this promise Abraham had no children. This is what God said to him, 'Your descendants will live in a foreign country, where they will be slaves and will be badly treated for four hundred years. But I will pass judgment on the people that they serve,' God said, 'and afterward they will come out of that country and will worship me in this place.' Then God gave to Abraham the ceremony of circumcision as a sign of the covenant. So Abraham circumcised Isaac a week after he was born; Isaac circumcised Jacob, and Jacob circumcised the twelve patriarchs.

"The patriarchs were jealous of Joseph, and sold him to be a slave in Egypt. But God was with him, and brought him safely through all his troubles. When Joseph appeared before Pharaoh, the king of Egypt, God gave him a pleasing manner and wisdom. Pharaoh made Joseph governor over the country and the royal household. Then there was a famine in all of Egypt and Canaan, which caused much suffering. Our ancestors could not find any food. So when Jacob heard that there was grain in Egypt, he sent his sons, our ancestors, on their first visit there. On the second visit Joseph made himself known to his brothers, and Pharaoh came to know about Joseph's family. So Joseph sent a message to his father, Jacob, telling him and the whole family to come to Egypt; there were seventy-five people in all. Then Jacob went down to Egypt, where he and our ancestors died. Their bodies were moved to Shechem, where they were buried in the grave which Abraham had bought from the tribe of Hamor for a sum of money.

"When the time drew near for God to keep the promise he had made to Abraham, the number of our people in Egypt had grown much larger. At last a different king, who had not known Joseph, began to rule in Egypt. He tricked our people and was cruel to our ancestors, forcing them to put their babies out of their homes, so that they would die. It was at this time that Moses was born, a very beautiful child. He was brought up at home for three months, and when he was put out of his home the daughter of Pharaoh adopted him and brought him up as her own son. He was taught all the wisdom of the Egyptians, and became a great man in words and deeds.

When Moses was forty years old he decided to visit his fellow Israelites. He saw one of them being mistreated by an Egyptian; so he went to his help and took revenge on the Egyptian by killing him. (He thought that his own people would understand that God was going to use him to set them free; but they did not understand.) The next day he saw two Israelites fighting, and he tried to make peace between them. 'Listen, men,' he said, 'you are brothers; why do you mistreat each other?' But the one who was mistreating the other pushed Moses aside. 'Who made you ruler and judge over us?' he asked. 'Do you want to kill me, just as you killed that Egyptian yesterday?' When Moses heard this he fled from Egypt and started living in the land of Midian. There he had two sons.

After forty years had passed, an angel appeared to Moses in the flames of a burning bush in the desert near Mount Sinai. Moses was amazed by what he saw, and went near the bush to look at it closely. But he heard the Lord's voice: 'I am the God of your ancestors, the God of Abraham, Isaac, and Jacob.' Moses trembled with fear and dared not look. The Lord said to him, 'Take your sandals off, for the place where you are standing is holy ground. I have looked and seen the cruel suffering of my people in Egypt. I have heard their groans, and I have come down to save them. Come now, I will send you to Egypt.'

"Moses is the one who was rejected by the people of Israel. 'Who made you ruler and judge over us?' they asked. He is the one whom God sent as ruler and savior, with the help of the angel who appeared to him in the burning bush. He led the people out of Egypt, performing miracles and wonders in Egypt and the Red Sea, and in the desert for forty years. Moses is the one who said to the people of Israel, 'God will send you a prophet, just as he sent me, who will be of your own people.' He is the one who was with the people of Israel assembled in the desert; he was there with our ancestors and with the angel who spoke to him on Mount Sinai; he received God's living messages to pass on to us.

"But our ancestors refused to obey him; they pushed him aside and wished that they could go back to Egypt. So they said to Aaron, 'Make us some gods who will go in front of us. We do not know what has happened to that Moses who brought us out of Egypt.' It was then that they made an idol in the shape of a calf, offered sacrifice to it, and had a feast to celebrate what they themselves had made. But God turned away from them, and gave them over to worship the stars of heaven, as it is written in the book of the prophets,

'People of Israel! It was not to me
that you slaughtered and sacrificed animals
for forty years in the desert.
It was the tent of the god Moloch that you carried,
and the image of the star of your god Rephan;
they were idols that you had made to worship.
And so I will send you away beyond Babylon.'

"Our ancestors had the tent of God's presence with them in the desert. It had been made as God had told Moses to make it, according to the pattern that Moses had been shown. Later on, our ancestors who received the tent from their fathers carried it with them when they went with Joshua and took over the land from the nations that God drove out before them. And it stayed there until the time of David. He won God's favor, and asked God to allow him to provide a house for the God of Jacob. But it was Solomon who built him a house.

"But the Most High God does not live in houses built by men; as the prophet says,

'Heaven is my throne, says the Lord,
and earth is my footstool.
What kind of house would you build for me?
Where is the place for me to rest?
Did not I myself make all these things?'

"How stubborn you are! How heathen your hearts, how deaf you are to God's message! You are just like your ancestors: you too have always resisted the Holy Spirit! Was there any prophet that

your ancestors did not persecute? They killed God's
messengers, who long ago announced the coming
of his righteous Servant. And now you have be-
trayed and murdered him. You are the ones who
received God's law, that was handed down by angels
—yet you have not obeyed it!"

Peter Before the Council in Jerusalem
Acts 15:7-11

After a long debate Peter stood up and said, "My
brothers, you know that a long time ago God chose
me from among you to preach the message of Good
News to the Gentiles, so that they could hear and
believe. And God, who knows the hearts of men,
showed his approval of the Gentiles by giving the
Holy Spirit to them, just as he had to us. He made
no difference between us and them; he purified
their hearts because they believed. So then, why do
you want to put God to the test now by laying a
load on the backs of the believers which neither
our ancestors nor we ourselves were able to carry?
No! We believe and are saved by the grace of the
Lord Jesus, just as they are."

Paul's Message in Athens
Acts 17:22-31

Paul stood up in front of the meeting of the
Areopagus and said, "Men of Athens! I see that in
every way you are very religious. For as I walked
through your city and looked at the places where
you worship, I found also an altar on which is
written, 'To an Unknown God.' That which you

worship, then, even though you do not know it, is what I now proclaim to you. God, who made the world and everything in it, is Lord of heaven and earth, and does not live in temples made by men. Nor does he need anything that men can supply by working for him, since it is he himself who gives life and breath and everything else to all men. From the one man he created all races of men, and made them live over the whole earth. He himself fixed beforehand the exact times and the limits of the places where they would live. He did this so that they would look for him, and perhaps find him as they felt around for him. Yet God is actually not far from any one of us; as someone has said,

'In him we live and move and exist.'
It is as some of your poets have said,
'We too are his children.'
Since we are God's children, we should not suppose that his nature is anything like an image of gold or silver or stone, shaped by the art and skill of man. God has overlooked the times when men did not know, but now he commands all men everywhere to turn away from their evil ways. For he has fixed a day in which he will judge the whole world with justice, by means of a man he has chosen. He has given proof of this to everyone by raising that man from death!"

Paul's Farewell to Ephesus
Acts 20:17-35

Paul sent a message from Miletus to Ephesus, asking the elders of the church to meet him. When they arrived, he said to them, "You know how I spent the whole time I was with you, from the first day I arrived in the province of Asia. With all humility and many tears I did my work as the Lord's servant, through the hard times that came to me because of the plots of the Jews. You know that I did not hold back anything that would be of help to you as I preached and taught you in public and in your homes. To Jews and Gentiles alike I gave solemn warning that they should turn from their sins to God, and believe in our Lord Jesus. And now, in obedience to the Holy Spirit, I am going to Jerusalem, not knowing what will happen to me there. I only know that in every city the Holy Spirit has warned me that prison and troubles wait for me. But I reckon my own life to be worth nothing to me, in order that I may complete my mission and finish the work that the Lord Jesus gave me to do, which is to declare the Good News of the grace of God.

"I have gone about among all of you, preaching the Kingdom of God. And now I know that none of you will ever see me again. So I solemnly declare to you this very day: if any of you should be lost, I am not responsible. For I have not held back from announcing to you the whole purpose of God. Keep watch over yourselves and over all the flock which the Holy Spirit has placed in your care. Be shepherds of the church of God, which he made his own through the death of his own Son. I know that after I leave, fierce wolves will come among you, and they will not spare the flock. The time will come when some men from your own group will tell lies to lead the believers away after them. Watch, then, and remember that with many tears, day and night, I taught every one of you for three years.

"And now I place you in the care of God and the message of his grace. He is able to build you up and give you the blessings he keeps for all his people. I have not coveted anyone's silver or gold or clothing. You yourselves know that with these hands of mine I have worked and provided everything that my companions and I have needed. I have shown you in all things that by working hard in this way we must help the weak, remembering the words that the Lord Jesus himself said, 'There is more happiness in giving than in receiving.' "